PHYSICAL DISABILITIES AND MEDICAL CONDITIONS

John Cornwall and

Christopher Robertson

David Fulton Publishers
London

David Fulton Publishers Ltd
Ormond House, 26–27 Boswell Street, London WC1N 3JD

First published in Great Britain by David Fulton Publishers 1999

Note: The right of John Cornwall and Christopher Robertson to be identified as the authors of this work has been asserted by them in accordance with the Copyright, Designs and Patents Act 1988

Copyright © John Cornwall and Christopher Robertson 1999

British Library Cataloguing in Publication Data
A catalogue record for this book is available from the British Library

ISBN 1–85346–525–9

Typeset by Textype Typesetters, Cambridge
Printed in Great Britain by Bell and Bain Ltd, Glasgow

Contents

Acknowledgements   Page iv

Introduction   Page v

Inclusion and equality of opportunity: where do IEPs fit in?   Page 1

	Principles	**Institutional self-review**	**Ideas for action**
IEPs, social and medical issues	Pages 11 to 17	Pages 18 to 19	
Individual and environmental assessment	Pages 20 to 27	Page 28	Pages 29 to 35
Targets, strategies and adjustments	Pages 36 to 42	Pages 43 to 46	Pages 47 to 50
Coordination and monitoring	Pages 51 to 60	Pages 61 to 64	Pages 65 to 70
Involving the learner	Pages 71 to 79	Pages 80 to 82	Pages 83 to 85
Partnership with parents	Pages 86 to 92	Pages 93 to 94	
Training	Pages 95 to 98	Page 99	Page 100 to 104

References   Page 105

Acknowledgements

This book results from work undertaken as part of a research project commissioned by the DfEE and managed at the Special Needs Research and Development Centre of the Department of Education at Canterbury Christ Church College of Education.

The views represented in this book are those of the authors and are not intended to represent the views or policies of any particular body, school or LEA. The authors would like to express their thanks to teachers, officers and staff in the following LEAs and schools whose work and provision has contributed, directly or indirectly, to this book.

Bolling Special School, Bradford
Cathcart Street Primary School, The Wirral
Kent Education Authority
Pendower Hall School, Newcastle-upon-Tyne
Raynehurst Infant and Junior Schools,
Twydall County Primary and Infant Schools, Gillingham
Valence School, Westerham

In particular, the authors would like to acknowledge the continued discussion with and co-operation and assistance from:

Dr Christine Barton (Equal Opportunities Consultant), Sheffield
Jenny Cobb, Education Consultant and former Head of Hospital School Services
Roland Gooding (Head) and Pat Thomas (Communication and Curriculum Access), Valence School
Mike Randall (Head), Cathcart Street Primary School, Merseyside
Lindsay Rousseau and Jan Molloy (Kent Physical and Sensory Impaired Services)
Aileen Webber (Author and Education Consultant), Cambridge
Ros Wells (Head Teacher), East Kent Hospital School Service

Introduction

This book is part of a series of books on individual education plans (IEPs), each focused on a specific aspect of special educational needs (SEN) and intended to support effective practices in mainstream schools working to make their provision inclusive. It is recommended that readers also explore the first book in the series, by Tod *et al.* (1998), *Implementing Effective Practice*. It is necessary to this volume in that it extends the generic work on IEPs and is complementary to this book and to the others in the series. It answers more general questions about the structure of IEPs and strategies emanating from them. This book uses a similar generic structure but focuses specifically upon the needs of and opportunities for pupils with physical disabilities and medical conditions. We start by asking some very basic questions in order to establish some principles upon which to base further IEP development work. Pupils with physical disabilities were often the first to be integrated into mainstream provision (Moses *et al.* 1988) because it was thought that the extent of the provision would be a welfare assistant for personal needs, some adaptation to furniture and equipment and some ramps to make the buildings accessible. This is not the case. Pupils with medical conditions or illness, on the other hand, did not figure highly in legislation and national planning until this decade (e.g. the legal basis for hospital school services changed with the implementation of the 1993 Education Act). Now there are growing hospital school services, emanating from former hospital schools, which are sharing their particular expertise with mainstream schools. There are many questions and issues raised by pupils whose disabilities or medical needs cause difficulties for them in educational environments.

Inclusion and equality of opportunity: where do IEPs fit in?

Issues of inclusion go well beyond the confines of the classroom. Inclusion is a 'societal' thing – not an educational slogan. The more we delve into the nature of the barriers to achievement, the more they become linked to choice, opportunity and strategies for learning (Cornwall 1995, 1996) than to the previous focus on the characteristics of physical conditions, the medical condition itself or selective physical access issues. The basic model for equality of opportunity encompasses the *attitudes of others towards an individual*, the physical environment and *procedures and practices* in daily working life (see Figure 1). They are all interconnected and complementary to each other, but catering for medical and therapeutic needs and providing an adequate physical environment does not necessarily provide equality of opportunity in learning.

Supporting learning requires attention to the development of the whole person (Rieser and Mason 1992, Cornwall 1995) and not just to 'bits that don't work'. It is an opportunity to examine the learning environment (including peer support and adult attitudes) as well as to plan for the skills a young person needs to learn, in order to achieve and to maintain their place in adult society. The difficulties faced by pupils labelled in this way are very often as much to do with the social and procedural environment as with any of the medical or physical difficulties they may experience. Thomas (1997, p. 106) describes the consequences of segregation in schools during this century as producing:

> a more academic curriculum . . . less flexible pastoral systems . . . in a system which is less familiar with and less accepting of difference and diversity.

For example, a child may not be able to go out to play every day because there are not enough staff available, read notices that are important because the notice board is too high or complete their work satisfactorily because they use alternative communication systems and there is too little time. The inflexibility of the education system as a whole has had to make

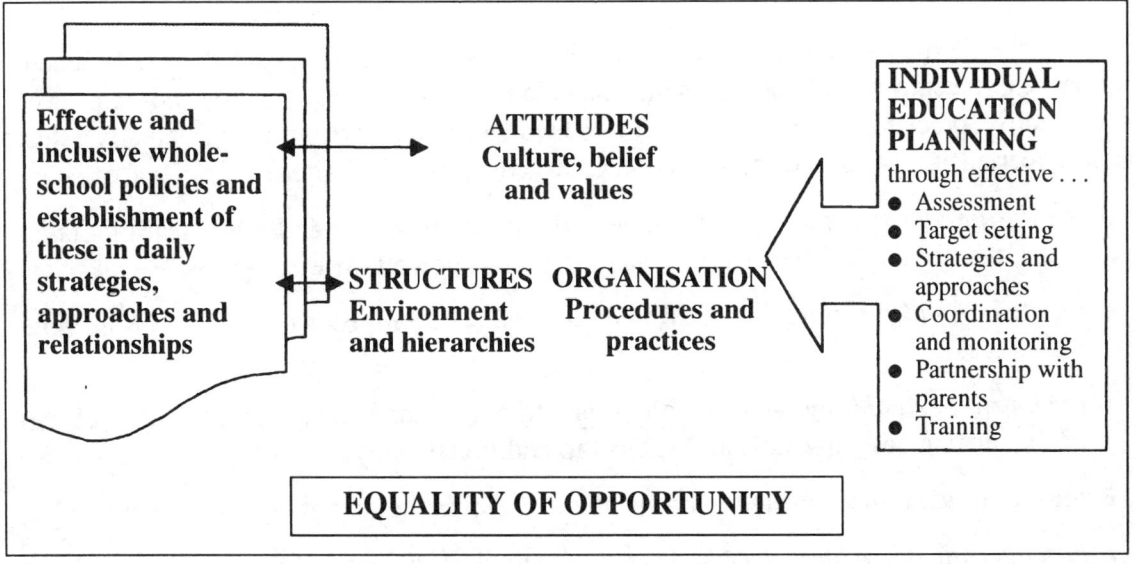

Figure 1

some pupils 'special' in order to cater for them at all. Traditionally, special education was seen as a specialised wing of the education system which took responsibility for a designated group of children. The assumption was that because of their disabilities or limitations these children required forms of education different from that offered to the majority. The aim was to provide forms of teaching that would overcome the problems of the children (Thomas 1997). The 'medicalisation' of special needs and particularly physical disabilities has left something of a legacy over the past 50 years. For example, it fragmented children into constituent parts dealt with by separate professionals (Cornwall 1995, chapters 1 and 2); it defined a limited range of expertise and excluded many people from positive action; and it left special schools open to criticism from Her Majesty's Inspectorate for providing too narrow a curriculum, insufficient challenge, low expectations, limited collaboration and poor assessment and record keeping. The Code of Practice (Department for Education (DfE), 1994) has been of benefit in clarifying the process of identifying SEN but has been, in other ways, a retrograde step. It has again placed children into a limited set of categories in contrast to the broad view of the diversity of needs inherent in the Warnock Report (1978). There are problems associated with regarding children as 'special' and putting them into such categories:

- it can be a strategic ploy to exclude pupils who might be regarded as difficult to teach or disruptive to the smooth running of the class or school;

- the pupil's educational experience can become narrowed and focused on deficits and problems rather than capability and progress;

- labelling on the basis of shared characteristics is discriminatory and encourages stereotypes that are disadvantageous to the pupils involved;

- it is often difficult for pupils in 'special' facilities to get back into mainstream life on leaving school.

Pupils in schools have a wide range of needs. Some pupils have been segregated from mainstream education, in the past because of medical or psychological characteristics and 'priority need' defined only by the kind of provision that was available.

Target setting, in both mainstream and special schools, will take explicit account of the scope for improving the achievements of children with SEN.
(Department for Education and Employment (DfEE), 1998)

Equality of opportunity for pupils is also bound up with the effectiveness of the whole-school approaches, strategies and relationships illustrated in Figure 1. Some of the broad consequences of ineffective procedures and practices for individual pupils, and which particularly affect pupils experiencing physical disabilities or medical conditions, are (after Barton 1996, p. 64):

- *the design and structure of a timetable*, which dictate where and when learning takes place, the distances between classes and the time allowed to get about;

- *the layout and furniture in classrooms and the positioning of teaching and learning resources*;

- *the journey to and from school* (or the separation from the local community), which can be exhausting and miserable and subject to additional delays;

- *the lack of appropriate training for members of staff* in the school or college community;

- *bureaucratic procedures* that can fragment a pupil or student and his or her educational experiences (on top of the effect of any illness or disability).

The solution to these problems for pupils with medical conditions or physical disabilities lies not in the creation of a separate and individual plan to remedy the problems that the pupil has, but more in a concerted whole-school development where IEPs are:

- embedded;

- explicit;

- educational.

What is an IEP?

The response to this particular set of diverse learning needs should be through shared responsibility, problem solving or strategy development and partnership with parents. This should be supported by effective coordination and monitoring, which, in turn, are supported by open and flexible management, particularly in enabling appropriate training and staff development. Figure 2 illustrates how *IEPs work within a pupil's broad entitlement, not instead of it*. The IEP is not an alternative curriculum or a set of individual work tasks. It epitomises the *additional and extra provision* that pupils are entitled to as well as their general entitlement to the whole of the general school curriculum, its activities and its social opportunities. For example, all pupils use equipment to help them learn (test tubes, computers, weighing machines). Some pupils may need to use a communication aid (high-technology such as a light talker chameleon, or low-technology such as a sign board) to help them learn, too. This is not 'special' in principle. We all use equipment to help us with our daily tasks (cars, washing machines, bicycles) – they don't make us 'special'. No, they are simply additional and extra equipment in the class or school. So it is important that attitudes, procedures and the learning environment as a whole are all considered – just as much as the shape and scope of the actual IEP – to ensure equality of educational opportunity. We therefore need to deal with the whole IEP process at two levels.

1. *The level of whole-school and regular in-class provision.* This comprises provision that is not organised specifically for one pupil. For example, procedures for dealing with the administration of medication are not *'additional and extra' provision for one pupil*; they are school-wide procedures. The more effective the procedures, the greater the diversity of pupils and circumstances they will include. This is efficiency. Having a school that is accessible to wheelchair users is not for one pupil but for all wheelchair users (including parents and, perhaps, governors or visiting professionals). Pupils with disabilities or medical conditions have a right to

   - all aspects of the physical environment;

   - a relevant and appropriate set of activities (timetable);

   - equal opportunity to gain knowledge and skills;

   - equal opportunity to use learning resources;

   - equal opportunity for success, academically and socially.

2. *The 'additional and extra' provision (including procedures, strategies and resources)* for an individual pupil. This is where the domain of the IEP comes into being. In Figure 2, we move from broadly based whole-school strategies to more detailed strategies and resources focused upon the needs of an individual. The importance of this view lies in the fact that the more effective the procedures and inclusive attitudes in place through whole-school approaches, the fewer individualised practices and resources will have to be accommodated. This is more efficient. The more inclusive a school is in its attitudes,

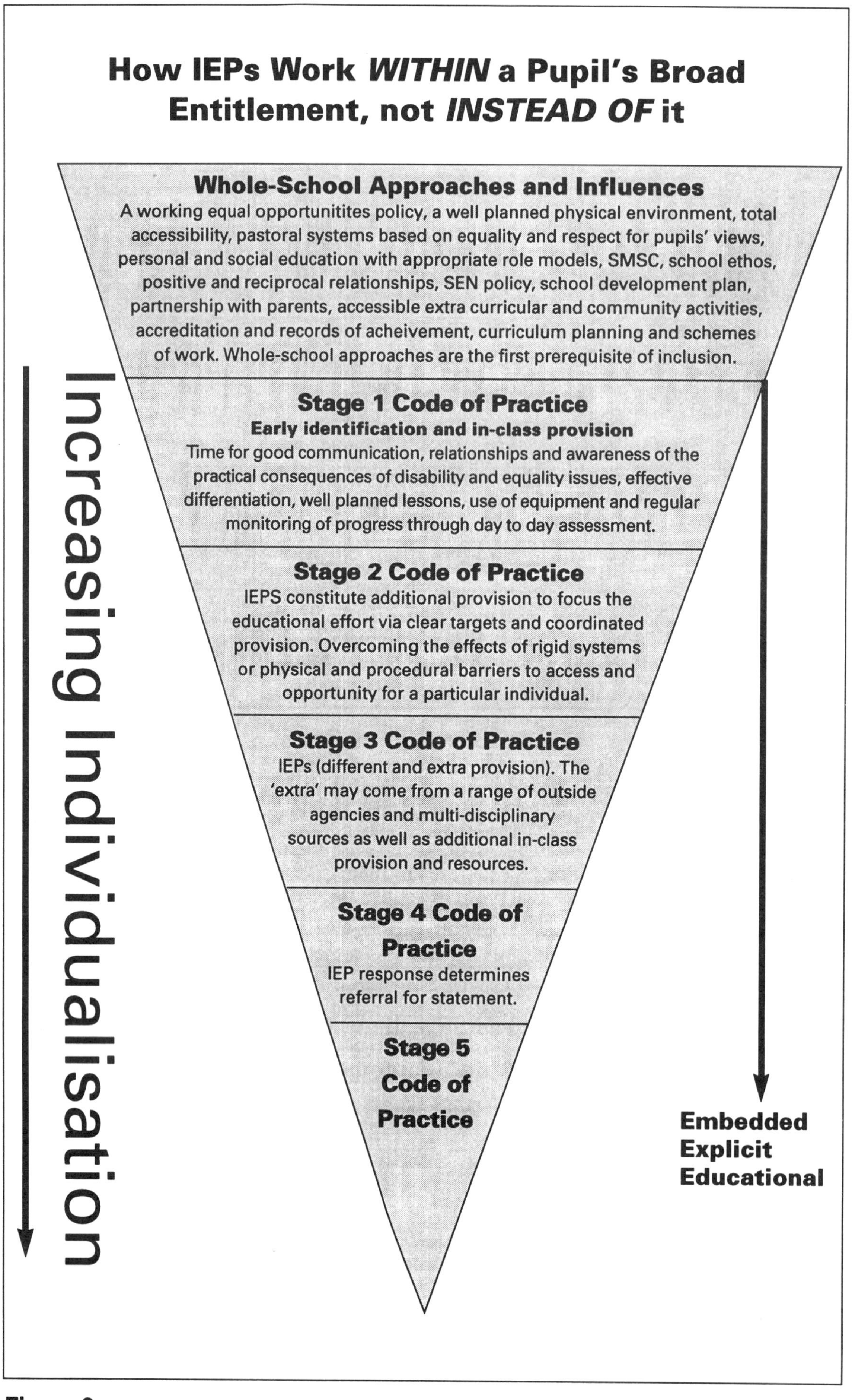

How IEPs Work *WITHIN* a Pupil's Broad Entitlement, not *INSTEAD OF* it

Increasing Individualisation

Whole-School Approaches and Influences
A working equal opportunitites policy, a well planned physical environment, total accessibility, pastoral systems based on equality and respect for pupils' views, personal and social education with appropriate role models, SMSC, school ethos, positive and reciprocal relationships, SEN policy, school development plan, partnership with parents, accessible extra curricular and community activities, accreditation and records of acheivement, curriculum planning and schemes of work. Whole-school approaches are the first prerequisite of inclusion.

Stage 1 Code of Practice
Early identification and in-class provision
Time for good communication, relationships and awareness of the practical consequences of disability and equality issues, effective differentiation, well planned lessons, use of equipment and regular monitoring of progress through day to day assessment.

Stage 2 Code of Practice
IEPS constitute additional provision to focus the educational effort via clear targets and coordinated provision. Overcoming the effects of rigid systems or physical and procedural barriers to access and opportunity for a particular individual.

Stage 3 Code of Practice
IEPs (different and extra provision). The 'extra' may come from a range of outside agencies and multi-disciplinary sources as well as additional in-class provision and resources.

Stage 4 Code of Practice
IEP response determines referral for statement.

Stage 5 Code of Practice

Embedded Explicit Educational

Figure 2

organisation, procedures and physical environment, the fewer completely individual and time-consuming strategies and procedures will be necessary. The 'additional and extra' will then become truly focused on what that individual really needs – not what he or she in common with 50 other pupils needs. For an obvious example, a wheelchair user may need an adjustable-height table. Having an adjustable-height table can be for other wheelchair users, later, and even for other uses in the school (e.g. computer work with touch screens or alternative keyboards) or for display purposes.

Figure 2 illustrates the broad provision and curriculum that all pupils are entitled to and emphasises that 'additional and extra' provision is not an alternative curriculum or 'instead of' a mainstream curriculum or a separate experience to mainstream school, but is *within a pupil's broad entitlement* while at school.

The Code of Practice (2:93) defines an IEP as setting out:

- the nature of the child's learning difficulty;
- action: the special needs provision; staff involved, including the frequency of support; at Stage 3, external specialists involved, including frequency and timing; specific programmes, activities, materials and equipment;
- help from parents at home;
- targets to be achieved in a given time;
- monitoring and assessment arrangements;
- review arrangements and date.

There are several problems and opportunities associated with the *pupil's curriculum entitlement, opportunities to involve broader strategies and the involvement of pupil and parents*. A more detailed discussion of these can be found in Tod *et al.* (1998) and Cornwall and Tod (1998).

Some initial questions about IEPs for pupils experiencing disabilities or medical conditions

- What is the *purpose* of IEPs generally and particularly for pupils with disabilities or medical conditions?
- Is the IEP an accounting activity or genuinely designed to *generate new learning*? Do targets have to be limited to areas defined in, say, the pupil's statement?
- *Is it educational* (through monitoring and evaluating learning) or administrative? Does it serve only to justify additional resources or adaptations?
- Should IEPs exist only to *provide access* to the main curriculum or should they be *part of a wider curriculum*?
- Are they to do with a pupil's own *longer-term personal, social and academic development*?
- *What is the role of the teachers or learning support assistants*? Have issues of passivity and enablement been thoroughly considered by all staff and the pupils concerned?
- Does it (and should it) include *pastoral supervision, counselling or therapies*? To what extent should targets be purely educational? Are there rational dividing lines?
- Are IEPs *limited* to specific skill targets (e.g. will use a touch talker . . .) without due concern for how *progress in those skills is actively evidenced* in everyday work and leisure (e.g. communicating weekend 'news' . . .)?

- Are targets set within *context, communication and discussion* with colleagues and pupil as recommended in the Code of Practice (and including external agencies/professionals)?

- Can individual targets be meaningful without considerable attention and adjustment to the physical and social (learning) environment?

- Are both the *pupils and parents* being given proper opportunities and encouragement to be fully involved?

- *Has there been training* to understand the nature of disabilities encountered and the consequences of the environment, attitudes and practices, and to understand the nature of empowerment and support for pupils' personal and academic achievements?

- Is the *curriculum used effectively* to work on issues of equality of opportunity, equal rights, disability issues and perceptions of illness and disability in society, empowerment, human rights and civil rights without personalising these?

Clearly, there are gains for both pupils and teachers when effective planning enables progress to be achieved and recognised. The IEP process should be integral to meeting individual needs, nurturing professional development and supporting whole-school development. Teachers report that IEPs have:

- provided a vehicle for the development of collaboration and involvement with parents and a mechanism for enabling pupils to become more involved in their own learning plans;

- directed teacher attention towards the setting and resetting of clear educationally relevant targets;

- involved all staff in the development and implementation of strategies to meet those targets and provided further opportunities for staff development;

- harnessed available material and human resources to meet those strategies through focused and coordinated 'educational' effort;

- increased the emphasis on monitoring and evaluating pupils' response to teaching in terms of progress;

- provided clearer evidence as to the effectiveness of additional SEN provision.

Possible difficulties teachers have identified (Tod *et al.* 1998) are as follows.

- The *written* IEP is not translated into practice. It thus becomes a cumbersome paperwork exercise which results in little educational benefit for the pupil.

- If SENCO takes on a major administrative role then his/her expertise in SEN teaching and coordination is not being used effectively.

- The IEP procedure is at risk of being used as an instrument for securing increased resources via 'evident failure'. This has been termed the 'perverse incentive'.

- An adherence to an objectives model of teaching via the writing of clear targets (Specific, Manageable, Achievable, Relevant, Timed (SMART)) may lead to a narrowing of learning opportunities for SEN pupils.

- The simplification of the IEP procedure via checklists, strategy banks and use of the commercial 'IEP' schemes could lead back to remediation via deficit rather than addressing individual needs.

- Difficulties in monitoring effectiveness of IEPs are such that there is a risk that IEPs will remain static documents or become so simplified that the educational benefit is questionable.

In short, the key question is what should be included in the IEP?

Ultimately, this question can only be fully answered with respect to any one individual and the school or learning context they are in. However, it is important to bear in mind the context of the pupil as well as the requirements for learning and access to the curriculum and social life of the school. This is how the social and educational objectives can work together to achieve a greater degree of *equality of opportunity* for pupils with physical disabilities or medical conditions. This is the main theme of this book and the details of planning with some suggestions and checklists are proffered to support the vital collaborative decision making that will take place over each IEP in the planning and monitoring of progress. An IEP can become a potent interactive tool that will open out possibilities for pupils, challenge inequalities in the system and highlight discrimination. In the bid to plan for effective inclusion and participation in school life, the IEP can highlight areas for whole-school development and provide opportunities to re-examine attitudes and practices that require development. It is, of course, an 'individualised' planning tool that offers extra and different support for a pupil who has physical or medical needs.

Why are IEPs for pupils with physical disabilities and medical conditions different from other areas of SEN?

The teacher's professional training, the requirements of the curriculum and time allocation make it impossible for them to act as surrogate parents, counsellors, practising psychologists or communication, speech, language, physical or occupational therapists or to become generators of social change in challenging the inequalities of the education system. The professional skills of a teacher include an awareness of the role of the IEP in establishing where progress is not occurring and the collaborative skills to engage colleagues and professionals from other disciplines where appropriate. Teachers have reported particular difficulties associated with developing and using IEPs for pupils with physical disabilities and medical conditions. There are three general manifestations of these barriers to learning experienced by pupils with physical disabilities or medical conditions.

- The *procedural and organisational barriers to cooperation and knowledge*. These range from the hitherto profound health, social and educational divisions in the management of professional services to the difficulties in a large comprehensive with many departments.

- The second manifestation comes with what are described as the 'additional or special' needs of this group of pupils in a limited definition of the physical resources for pupil needs e.g. communication aids (high- and low-technology systems), physical adaptations (wheelchairs, ramps, walkers, laptops) or the skills and knowledge needed, for example, in the administering of drugs or therapy. It is *the use of adaptations not their existence* which defines them as a *resource*.

- Thirdly, the competitive striving for image and success in the nature of modern schooling reflects society generally, and creates an environment where children 'with difficulties' are necessarily 'special'. *General attitudes, prejudices, stresses on teachers and expectations of individuals* and the school as a whole become factors that will affect a pupil's progress.

The barriers to cooperation often stem from the ways in which the respective services are managed, compounded by professional boundaries and the need for credibility or status. Where the barriers to cooperation between services have been compensated for by staff on the ground or by forward-looking management, there is pupil centred and flexible provision enabling the pupil to experience a coherent flow of educational and life activities. Where they have not, there is often inflexible and adult or professional role centred provision in which the adult attitudes and professional ideologies compete with each other for space in the pupil's educational and life experiences – usually to the detriment of their education and social opportunities.

Teachers may feel that coping with physical and medical problems is outside their professional competence and thus they feel unnecessarily insecure. They see the medical or health expertise as being dominant and sometimes struggle to identify the educational domains in which these pupils' opportunities reside. As a consequence, there has been a tendency for IEPs for pupils with physical disabilities or medical conditions to risk becoming:

- Individual, separate and isolated, concerned solely with deficits within the child;

- Exclusive and separated from usual practice or long-term achievement;

- Planning which is static and does not trigger a dynamic process.

When this occurs, teachers find themselves with additional tasks with which they may not feel secure and which often do not result in progress towards meaningful educational objectives. For example, it is sometimes difficult to see how a teacher's role in helping a child with diabetes can be integrated into their own personal and social development programme, for instance taking responsibility for their own medication as a longer-term goal. Once the requirements of pupils with disabilities or medical conditions can be seen as part of both personal and curricular work, then teachers and support assistants can develop a meaningful *educational perspective and role* with such pupils.

There have to be adjustments and adaptations to the school system, including IEPs, as well as a clear definition of an educational approach and the limits of a teacher's responsibilities. This book supports a positive approach to teaching and classroom management skills and whole-school development. It encompasses an educational approach to helping pupils with physical disabilities or medical conditions and to advancing their learning and academic progress through the use of IEPs, in the context of adjustments to the physical and social environment, and within a progressive and structured curriculum or longer-term plan for personal development. Teachers are skilled in and trained to promote learning, and learning is what is required for both academic achievement and personal development, social participation or independence. The IEP is an educational tool that can have a powerful impact on a pupil's progress. Much has been achieved as a consequence of the gains that schools have made to coordinate educational effort in getting IEPs up and running. However, to date, the static and often cumbersome written 'plan' has overshadowed the need to develop a manageable and focused 'process'. It would be unfortunate if, after 3 years of dynamic and collaborative development activity, the administrative burden of IEPs was allowed to occlude the benefits of applying the educational principles inherent in the philosophy of IEPs. This book seeks to build on the progress that your school has made so far by placing an emphasis on the monitoring and evaluation aspects of IEPs. It does this by focusing attention upon the benefits to pupils in terms of their educational progress.

Self-development activity

Table 1 might provide an opportunity for you to consider some basic principles with regard to your own approach.

	Teachers	Learning or special support staff	SENCO and school management team
What is the *purpose* of IEPs generally? Does this purpose include *physical and social adjustments*?			
What is the *purpose of IEPs for pupils with physical or medical conditions*?			
Are IEPs an accounting activity or genuinely designed to *generate new learning*?			
Are IEPs educational (through monitoring and evaluating learning) or administrative?			
Should IEPs exist only to *provide access* to the main curriculum or should they be *part of the whole curriculum*?			
What have they got to do with a pupil's own longer-term *personal development*?			
What is the role of the teachers or learning support assistant?			
Do they include *physical management*, counselling or therapies?			
Are targets set *within context, communication or discussion* as recommended in the Code of Practice?			
Are IEPs *limited* to individual skill targets without recognising the context of these targets?			
Are both *the pupils and the parents* being given proper opportunities and encouragement to be *fully involved*?			
Are opportunities to integrate curricular and personal development being taken (e.g. English and speech therapy; PE and physiotherapy)?			
Has there been *training to understand the social and educational context* for pupils with disabilities or medical needs?			

Table 1

Discussion points for institutional self-review

How do you/does your school view the problem?

Which set of responses is more useful in planning a way forward?

From an *individual* point of view (medical – the problem is in the child; negative; reliant on other expertise) or from a *socially* responsible and educational viewpoint where everyone can take part in educational developments (the problem belongs to us all). Use Table 2 as a basis for discussing how your provision reflects (not what you individually think) one or the other viewpoint.

Education provision and relationships	Medically based or individual view (problem in the pupil)	Educational or socially responsible view (problem in the context)
Accommodation	Cannot walk, cannot move around the building or classroom. Confined to wheelchair.	Badly designed building – no lifts or ramps. Wheelchair opens up more opportunity – a mobility aid.
Curriculum	Cannot take part in PE. Must have time out of lessons for medical treatment or therapy.	Inappropriate aims or content. Medical therapy requirements may conflict with the timetable.
Classroom	Cannot move about the classroom. Needs additional adult help.	Reluctance to accept additional resources and aids in the classroom. Classroom is not big enough.
Teaching and learning	Is difficult to teach. Cannot write or record work or communicate understanding/knowledge. Cannot work at the same speed as the rest of the class.	Lack of knowledge about differentiation and inclusive activities related to the curriculum. Need to be more creative in adaptations and environmental changes.
Resources	Cannot use the same curriculum materials. Needs a cure. Expensive special resources for only one pupil.	Lack of resources for, knowledge about or development of inclusive activities. Resources can be used by other pupils, too.
Personal and social	Needs tender loving care and lower expectations. Cannot attend to personal care. Cannot communicate with others. Walks slowly with aids.	Teacher expectations and superior attitudes are the problem. Lack of acceptance and belonging in the school community as a whole.

Adapted, with thanks, from Barton 1997.

Table 2

IEPs, social and medical issues: Principles

It is worthwhile looking at some overall principles and ideas that are currently guiding educational and social philosophies towards pupils with physical disabilities and medical conditions. Despite the title of this book, the two so-called categories of pupils are not the same. Within each of these categories, defined in the Code of Practice, there is such a widely differing variety of needs, abilities, circumstances and characteristics as to make almost a nonsense of them. In the following chapters, it should be remembered that advice and guidance of this sort relate to general features and are intended to generate a systematic, sensitive and positive response to the kind of problems found. This is not a detailed, prescriptive manual of actions you should take in any specific case. 'Rules' and legislation offer, at best, an overall vision of the long-term direction in which to move. They are not solutions in themselves and flexibility for individuals is of paramount importance.

The term 'inclusion' has to do with the whole context in which a person finds themselves. It is not about changing an individual, placing them in a mainstream school, making them 'better' or even providing special adaptations to survive in a physically hostile environment. It is about attitudes, whole-school approaches and reasonable adjustments to the school environment. The *physical adjustments*, while often necessary, may not have as much impact for a pupil as *the procedural and attitudinal changes* necessary to make a reasonable environment for a pupil with disabilities or medical conditions.

The UN standard rule below sets out a vision of equal opportunity for children and young people with disabilities in a system where they are 'an integral part'. It espouses the view that all children are entitled to the support they need in order to maintain their rightful place in their own school community. These rules are challenging but they cannot be realised until teachers, learning support staff, therapists and other professionals are able to clarify the quality of support and the appropriateness and sufficiency of resources. It raises the question of what 'an integral part' of the education system really means.

UN standard rules – disability
Rule 6: education

States should recognise the principle of equal primary, secondary and tertiary educational opportunities for children, youth and adults with disabilities, in integrated settings. They should ensure that the education of persons with disabilities is an integral part of the educational system.

I. General educational authorities are responsible for the education of persons with disabilities in integrated settings. Education for persons with disabilities should form an integral part of national educational planning, curriculum development and school organisation.

2. Education in mainstream schools presupposes the provision of interpreter and other appropriate support services. Adequate accessibility and support services, designed to meet the needs of persons with different disabilities, should be provided. Persons with disabilities should be involved in the education process at all levels.

The following two standpoints on teaching and learning provide a useful starting point. One is now rather out of date and seen as less useful in educational terms and the second is now becoming more prominent and regarded as more inclusive. They are:

- *an individual or remedial type model of implementing IEPs*;

- *. . . more of a social and educational model.*

An individual or remedial type model of implementing IEPs expects the problem to reside solely within the child and the 'remedy' to be situated there too. This has also been called the 'medical model' (Stone 1985, Halliday 1989, Barnes 1991, Jones 1992, Mason and Rieser 1994, Cornwall 1995). There is the implication that:

- the only thing that needs to change is something *'within the child'* – often this is patently impossible;

- once the 'treatment' or intervention is completed, everything will revert to normal – there is *little regard for broader evaluation or maintenance*;

- the remedy *relies solely on the expertise of others* outside the classroom and sometimes the school;

- *implementation causes problems for all* – of availability, timetabling and equality of opportunity for the pupil;

- *the pupil may be stigmatised* by having to have special treatment or education with its attendant discomfort and sometimes social ridicule;

- it may also become narrow in its focus *and not be related to the broader needs of the pupil* both in school and beyond school *or the teacher(s)*;

- it may relate solely to limited skills useful only in the classroom or in a specific setting and *cannot be usefully generalised to broader situations*;

- it is related to particular ideologies and *treatments promoted by those with vested interests* inside or outside the school;

- the programme will not necessarily be evaluated in terms of long-term benefits to the pupil and will leave you with *the problem of 'where to go from here'* once the limited targets have been achieved.

At the end of the day, all of the pressure on the pupil to achieve and on the mechanics of, say, seating or alternative communication systems makes little recognition of the fact that inclusion is a contract with the context and surroundings. The total beneficial effect of correct seating will be undermined if the pupil becomes isolated in one corner of the classroom with much reduced contact with peers. The most advanced communication system in the world is of little value if there are no 'communication partners', friends and stimulating conversations to be had. Sometimes, a concentration on intervening or giving undue attention to the mechanics of furniture, positioning, treatments and classroom organisation can militate against a positive overall view of inclusion as 'acceptance, community and belonging' (Forest and Pearpoint 1991).

The use of therapies and alternative communication systems, for example, is very important to a pupil's general quality of life and such systems should be well coordinated but they are not, strictly, educational strategies or suitable for setting curricular and individualised learning targets. They provide additional support and access to learning, to the curriculum activities on offer and to participation in the general life of the school and community. Arguably, some targets related to these areas are more to do with the daily management of the pupil, from an adult perspective, than a genuine part of the pupil's educational development in the short-, medium- or long-term.

Pupils may need multi-agency and sometimes one-to-one support

Such an arrangement may well require additional help in a number of different forms, such as a personal support worker, regular physiotherapy or speech therapy, visits from a specialist teacher and the use of items of equipment and adapted materials, all of which will be provided to enable the learner to access the curriculum. The extent of the partnerships around him or her, necessary in order to participate in educational opportunity, are complex but acceptance means not seeing them as a 'problem'. For example, a teacher may welcome a pupil who has missed a significant amount of school through illness with a 'run down' on all the areas they have missed; depending on how sensitively it is done, it only reinforces the difficulties and undermine confidence. Perhaps the first step is to welcome the pupil back and allow them time to settle now they are well again?

The greater the impairment, the greater the level of paid intervention and the greater is the potential fragmentation of personal development from an early age. Taking on this paradox requires the professionals to engage in a process of problem solving *'with' the pupil, student or client, rather than 'to' or 'at' the pupil.* It requires an acknowledgement of the *source of control* of the process. *This belongs with the pupil, student or client.* They are accessing the services of the professional, not vice versa. An appropriate attitude towards personal independence sometimes comes about without, or despite, the direct intervention of an array of paid or professional enablers.

It is also important in the midst of the multi-professional activities to *maintain a clear educational perspective.* This is not always easy as different priorities will be competing for valuable time and a young person can easily become fragmented into a sum of his or her parts, defined by the professionals. Partnerships and inclusion mean that the young person and their parents will have the guiding hand and will make the salient decisions about life and educational opportunity based on sound advice from the various professionals, working together – not competing for time, money, acknowledgement of their professional credibility and other irrelevant pressures. *In terms of IEPs*, it is vital that teachers and learning support staff keep their eye firmly on the ball – that is, *the educational targets and aims* that give medium-

and longer-term purpose to the activities undertaken. Mobility (walking, sitting, standing) is not necessarily any use if there is nowhere to go and nothing worthwhile to 'sit up and pay attention' to. It is of use to get to the shops or to queue alongside your peers to make a choice of lunch dishes at a self-service canteen. Independence skills (e.g. telling the time, managing money, etc.) are of no use at all unless you are truly given the opportunity to use them in making choices and authoritative decisions and in controlling important aspects of your life.

A good example of this is in work done to achieve so-called 'independence'. For many years it was thought to be sufficient to teach 'independence skills', in short, how to look after yourself, how to deal with daily domestic problems and how to manage your money. This kind of approach automatically leads to reduced expectations. If you can't do it for yourself, then you can't function. A more positive *educational* view is to develop targets, strategies and curricular activities that are part of the overall learning process – new ways of looking at these problems, which have, in the last 10 years, become more prevalent. *We all use aids and adaptations* (bicycles, cars, computers) and we all have other people doing things for us in different ways. If we can't plaster a wall, we get in someone who can. For someone who uses a wheelchair, *independence means being able to recruit or manage other people in an appropriate way to get the things* they need, done. *Independence means being able to muster the support you need when you need it* – not being able to do everything for yourself. The disabled individual's mobility is mediated by others. This affects the learning process, a large component of which is exploratory or active. The desire for independence is constantly frustrated, and there are inevitable strains (Prosser 1992).

It is these partnerships that can provide continuity and progression in learning for the child to the young adult. Herein lies the problem for a young person who may have grown up experiencing a predominance of professionally oriented relationships and whose natural support systems may have become subservient to professional intervention or negative social attitudes to their disability; for example:

- disabled people can't interact socially ('Does he take sugar?');

- we have to be cheerful;

- negative aversive attitudes of a person, such as authoritarianism, ego strength or body concern (from Prosser 1992).

Another problem is that of fragmentation of experience for the young person because of the different perspectives and activities of the professionals involved. They have to make sense of the various types of input they receive from physiotherapists and PE teachers, from speech and language therapists and from English teachers. This is not always easy and can involve considerable duplication of effort. Table 3 is a little simplistic as, in reality, there are many overlapping and merging areas of consideration between health professionals and teachers. The point that emerges is important nevertheless. Too much duplication of targets or argument about the nature and importance of specific targets can become counter-productive.

Historically, educational targets have been subservient to medical or health objectives, often to the point where teachers have become overwhelmingly concerned about them and not about knowledge, understanding and skill on a broader educational front. The targets are important and the task for teachers is to relate their targets to educational and social progress (see Figure 3). In this way they will complement, not duplicate, other targets and the work of other professionals.

There are many areas of common ground and overlap between the different professional perspectives illustrated by the potential targets or objectives that they are each aiming for. A child or young person does not function in any way akin to the division of professional responsibilities and bodies of knowledge. What is learned in speech and language therapy

Area of work	Possible health or medical targets – examples . . .	Related educational and social targets – examples . . .
Physiotherapy	• Reduction of asymmetric tonic (perhaps, neck) reflexes • Flexion and extension of fingers • Develop back muscle tone and confidence for sitting up • Holding up head successfully for 3 minutes	• Maintain balance on floor/mat or on box and walk forward (PE) • Use hands in simple movement (dance) or expressive movement • Gaining eye contact to work in a group
Speech and language therapy	• Articulating vowel sounds • Initiating a communication • Prescribing an aid for communication • Developing intentional communications	• Engaging in conversation and making friends • Asking for clarification of instructions in class • Evaluating the effectiveness of an aid or adaptation • Indicating which pencil grip is best
Occupational therapy	• Grasping and releasing an object • Developing successive levels of manual dexterity • (Prescribing aids and furniture to) maintain a fixed and balanced seating position	• Holding a pencil – picking it up if dropped on the desk • Using arm, finger or fist to select buttons (or use mouse) to control Information and Communications Technology (ICT) • Use adapted keyboard to record personal details and timetable
Medical	• Administration of medication • Tracking the progress of a medical condition • Recommended periods of rest • Checking health parameters (on referral or as routine) • Communicate the symptoms and prognosis of a condition	• Learn about, manage and control own medication • Understand their own disability or condition and consequences • Actively set own realistic targets on return to school or during illness

Table 3

may not be much different to the receiver to what is learned in English. The difficulty for the teacher and school is to be able to coordinate and *not replicate* this work, or the recording of progress, and waste much valuable time.

The explicit and educational nature of IEPs is examined later but first it is necessary to consider the basic social and medical influences that are likely to impact on progress but which are not necessarily educational or curricular targets themselves. In other words, they must not be forgotten – but do they constitute appropriate areas to develop learning targets for the pupil? There are no simple answers to this question – it is something that teachers and schools, together with their pupils and parents, will have to decide for themselves. Opting for more of a *social and educational model*, encompassing the relationship between the learner and his or her environment, the IEP will be equally concerned with how:

the particular needs of individual pupils and groups of pupils . . . are met within the teaching and the life of the school generally. (OFSTED framework 1992)

A number of good things have emerged from the 1993 Education Act and its subsequent Code of Practice, and these are clearly outlined in Cornwall and Tod (1998) and in Tod *et al.* (1998). The discussion is about the issues around both raising standards and inclusion and also about the mutual compatibility, in practice, of these two notions.

We now have the Green Paper, 'Excellence for all children (meeting special educational

The use of IEPs should be embedded and explicit and have a clear position within the context of a whole-school approach

SCHOOL MANAGEMENT:
- Institutional self-review
- Clear decisions/consensus (how and who in recording?)
- Agreeing key criteria and priorities
- Choosing appropriate methods

TARGET SETTING:
- Access, process and response targets
- Direct, flexible and indirect linkage targets (see pp. 36–50).

Various ways of building up . . .
RECORDING SYSTEMS AND EVIDENCE:
- Statements of achievement
- Comment banks
- Grading systems
- Progress grids
- Descriptive assessments
- Prescriptive assessments
- Self-assessment
- Physical evidence (photos, tapes)

MONITORING PROGRESS THROUGH IEPs Combining individual targets with environmental adjustments

TARGET CONTENT: Derived from various sources . . .
- Skills or sub-skills
- Course modules
- Developmental steps
- Other individual goals
- Group objectives
- Subjects/areas of knowledge
- Attitudes/personal aims
- Concepts and understanding

The effectiveness of IEPs will have
CONSEQUENCES for:
- The school ethos
- Pupil motivation
- Teaching styles
- Learning programmes
- Curriculum development
- Choice of systems
- Time and training

Figure 3

needs) . . .', which emphasises raising standards for all, including pupils with special needs, through inclusive educational practice and higher expectations and by working collaboratively with outside agencies. The challenge for this book is to examine issues, to suggest development for schools and also to highlight strategies for raising standards and including pupils and students with physical disabilities and medical conditions. In other words let's make them into 'green' and 'inclusive' IEPs, rather than IEPs that create a separate world for a child and do not allow for long-term social development, acceptance and a sense of belonging to an educational community, to the extent that if pupils with disabilities or medical conditions are not present, they will be sorely missed. This is an equal opportunity standpoint and is inclusive, characterised by adjustments to policies, management and arrangements both in the class and in the school generally. It will be concerned with the whole process of teaching and learning as an issue of access to the whole curriculum and to the learning resources needed. It should not resort to passing the responsibility for physical development or self-management over to other professionals or ignoring the necessity of the pupils' own responsibility to manage themselves, and others, effectively in order to learn.

Summary points

- *The purpose of IEPs is to enable the child to make progress* – not to change the child to fit the system or to leave purposeful strategies and activities in physical and personal development to extra-curricular provision or other professionals. Pupils with physical disabilities or medical conditions may or may not have the power directly to affect their conditions. More often than not they cannot directly or intentionally change their conditions and the school should not see them as the problem.

- *Teachers are experts in learning and **can** implement effective IEPs for pupils* with physical disabilities and medical conditions. These can be enhanced by positive attitudes encouraged through the curriculum and whole-school ethos.

- *Teachers cannot be expected to perform multi-professional functions* (i.e. therapy, counselling, parenting, social work, medical support, etc.). They should take responsibility for pupils' learning, progress and general well-being and should know how and when to refer pupils for additional professional or voluntary help. They should also be able to work collaboratively and expect or manage others to do so.

- *Learning support assistants (and teachers sometimes) need to become partners* in communication and in additional support for learning and encouraging real independence through choice and control. They are not used efficiently just as welfare helpers dealing solely with personal care needs.

- Teachers need to be aware that they have *an effect on pupils' personal and social development* and that this, in turn, affects pupil learning. This is particularly true for children with disabilities or medical conditions who may be prone to unfair treatment or bullying or to patronising attitudes with low expectations.

- IEPs need to be *explicit, embedded and educational* not complex, isolated and administrative.

- IEPs are most effective when they promote the *active involvement of pupil and parents* in the learning process and in the social life of the school.

- *The effectiveness of an IEP* should be judged not by the written individual education *plan* but by the *effect it has on pupils' progress* achieved through focused targets, increased participation and access to the curriculum.

- *Monitoring pupil response to the IEP is a key area* for development in schools. Often considerable adjustments need to be made to enable pupils to make effective responses to assessment, tests, etc. This is sometimes complex, involving a range of professionals from health and education with different training and different management systems.

- *IEPs have been a successful vehicle for addressing diversity* and involving all staff in SEN provision. The strength of the IEP lies in its effect on planning. It should not be abandoned simply because it is time-consuming and cumbersome; rather, it should be streamlined to be more efficient.

IEPs, social and medical issues: Institutional self-review

Place your IEPs on firm foundations . . .

These are general considerations for pupils with physical disabilities and medical conditions but also for pupils who may be experiencing difficulties related to any form of physical, sensory, medical or social problems interfering with their academic progress. Have you had the opportunity to audit or review the basic requirements of the Code of Practice in your school? Use a scale of 1–7 to rate your school or service in relation to the areas outlined in Table 4. You can use the 'comments' column to record why you have given it a high (or low) mark and perhaps discuss with colleagues to see how much you agree.

Code of practice	Your rating	Comments (e.g. why that score?)
Does the *IEP address any significant discrepancies* between the expectations of the child (by parents, external specialists and teachers) and the results of standardised tests, cognitive tests or National Curriculum (NC) tests?		
Is the teacher *able to account for and report* discrepancies between NC assessment results and what the pupil knows, understands and can do in daily class work with appropriate time and support?		
Have the parents and the school sought any *additional advice from voluntary bodies or specialist support*?		
Are there *constructive relationships* surrounding the pupil and do these include the *involvement of parents or carers*?		
Is there *consultation and open discussion* between the child's parents, the school, the school doctor or the pupil's general practitioner, the community paediatrician or any other specialist medical services involved?		
Has *external advice* been sought in developing a meaningful programme for the individual pupil and is this external advice *reflected in the pupil's IEP* or individual programme?		
Has a pro-active approach been adopted to involve the medical or therapy support *in advance of crisis points whenever possible*?		
Is information technology (IT) *used effectively to provide access to the curriculum* for pupils who find it hard to communicate, for example?		

Table 4

Compare your IEPs with the characteristics below and consider any possible adjustments

- It is rooted within the planning for all pupils within the class.

- It is positive in tone and pays due recognition to pupil strengths.

- It is social in context.

- It triggers a dynamic response to individual needs.

- It describes the 'extra and different' provision needed by the pupil in relation to provision made at Stage 1 of the Code of Practice. That is, it is not 'instead of' but *'additional to'*. Clearly it follows that if provision at whole-school level and at Stage 1 is effective the need for 'extra and different' is likely to be reduced.

- It seeks to harness available human and physical resources such that 'educational effort' is *coordinated* and *focused* towards the attainment of relevant and achievable targets.

- It is linked to the curriculum.

- It is comprehensible and can be implemented by those involved.

- It can be monitored regularly, evaluated and adjusted accordingly.

- It is based on an assessment of pupil progress.

- It seeks to move the pupil from 'what he can do' to 'what is expected'. Short-term target setting is linked to medium- and long-term objectives.

- Integral to planning is the acknowledgement that 'new' behaviours need to be consolidated and generalised.

- It reflects the active involvement of pupil and parent (guardian/carer).

Individual and environmental assessment: Principles

Some pupils begin their lives or early school careers with physical disabilities or a serious medical condition, while other pupils develop disabilities or conditions later in their school lives. Sometimes they are short-term, sometimes they are longer-term or permanent, and sometimes they may not be considered by some as a disability – for example, asthma, epilepsy, attention deficit hyperactivity disorder ADHD, disfigurement, mental illness or as having any impact on a pupil's capabilities and opportunities.

> Such difficulties may, *without action by the school or LEA* [local education authority], limit the child's access to the full curriculum. Some children with physical disabilities may also have sensory impairments, neurological problems and learning difficulties.
>
> (Code of Practice, 3:71, p. 6, original italics)

Assessment is important not only to establish individual needs and the need for adjustments to the learning environment and experiences of the pupil, but also to act as a way of sharing and communicating information. Teachers (and other professionals) are not the only ones who 'assess'. Everyone coming into contact with the child will make some form of assessment. Some may be ill-informed and peremptory and some well-considered and balanced. It is likely that the pupil will become aware of other people's assessments in the normal course of events.

A young disabled child will have a different experience to that of other children purely because the opportunities for movement and exploration will be hampered at a time when early experiences are being built up. Similarly, a child who has experienced serious or prolonged illness prior to school is likely to have missed out on much early learning experience – particularly in the important areas of developing social and learning skills. There may be a range of obstacles to early learning for a disabled child, depending upon the nature and severity of the disability (See next page).

On the other hand, a very young child gains their very early experience through the hands of parents and other adults. Being handled, carried and stimulated is an important part of development in the early years and it is just as important for a disabled child. There is no reason why parents cannot continue to stimulate and handle their young child and, in partnership with others, using knowledge gained, begin to compensate to some degree for the reduction in the child's experience of movement and space and, perhaps, their inability to communicate without assistance. There are additional stresses for parents and child that come from coping not just with physical or medical difficulties but with an inherently hostile physical (and sometimes social) environment. Once their infant has developed language (or has learned to communicate via alternative means), parents skilfully begin to change their communication style at times so as to prepare their child for school. Instead of merely communicating socially, the adult adopts a 'teaching style' approach and asks the child questions such as 'What colour are your shoes?' and 'How many plates do we need to put on the table?' Similarly, they move from seeking to establish 'joint attention' to developing the skill of having the child's attention directed by an adult: 'Let's make a nice picture to put on the fridge – hold the red pencil and draw me a lovely apple'. They also try to get their child to listen, and engage in school type activities: reading, drawing, numbers,

Early exploration and experience could be curtailed and less 'rich' through difficulties of moving about, or amongst people, and of handling or exploring new objects.

Eating and drinking can be very much more difficult and these early independence skills may be hampered, along with the all-important social and emotional needs that are fulfilled by them.

Continence is another early learning area that can become overwhelming depending upon cultural pressures exerted on parents (e.g. acceptance or stigmatisation).

Readiness for school may take longer, as will some of the pre-school skills, due to different physical experiences.

Discomfort, pain and fatigue are all experienced to varying degrees and can act as a disincentive to 'activity', including educational activity. A disabled child will have grown up with this and will have developed his or her own strategies for dealing with it.

Time spent being subjected to examination or scrutiny, medical or psychological; physiotherapy, speech therapy or even operations to correct posture and movement problems. The fragmentation of experience for a very young child can be considerable. 'Jumping through hoops' for a range of different people with no meaningful links has emotional consequences: 'Leave me alone . . .'.

Sleeping is sometimes a problem due to discomfort or pain (or sometimes physiotherapy treatments).

etc. Parents can often offer the one-to-one attention needed to support successful attempts to manipulate materials or to develop the physical stamina to be able to remain 'on task'. They encourage their child to make choices and to direct his/her own attention: 'What would you like to draw? Think about what colour you would like the roof to be. Can you be very clever and finish off the picture by yourself?' The important point to note is that these skills and the attendant experiential learning are explicitly taught and learned during the years prior to school entry. There is a tendency, particularly if the child has difficulties with communication, for adults to begin to take complete control of conversations and not to attempt to find a way to understand the child's (perhaps non-verbal) communications. It is very easy for adults to end up talking to themselves, with the child having given up completely – possibly not listening or paying attention. Often a great deal more time needs to be taken to ensure that communication is two-way. A child who is disabled or ill may well have to muster considerably more will and energy to perform simple tasks than his or her peers. The appearance of lethargy or apathy could simply be tiredness. The length of activities should be monitored in relation to the effects of the child's illness or disability, and the child's stamina built up accordingly.

Children with physical disabilities or serious medical conditions tend to miss out on a significant amount of these experiences and activities. If a child does not have these experiences, and arrives in school without the appropriate learning skills and organisational support, then he/she will not only make slower academic progress and have more peer-related problems, but will also have to acquire these experiences in a group setting where failure is public. For some children this physical and social delay can be addressed in school by using an available adult and selected peers to recreate successful communication in social situations and by thoroughly assessing how the social and physical context can be adjusted. Children seek to *make sense of their environment* and *protect themselves from further failure*. Medical diagnoses are based on deficiencies, problems or impairments whereas educational programmes are based on areas of development, growth, success and capability. This means taking into account medical and health (or therapy) needs and information but not basing the educational programme on them. No pupil is ill or disabled by choice and through considerable adjustments to the learning environment (attitudes, procedures and physical environment) may need to be made, *it is not the pupil who is the problem*. Teachers need to be able to decide whether the pupil's disability or illness has some elements that can be alleviated immediately or cured directly and how long this will take. On the other hand, it is as important to plan carefully for the necessary adjustments that need to be made to the physical and social environment which will facilitate progress and learning in the longer term. Teachers then need to plan and adjust strategies accordingly.

- It is necessary to ask 'Are we trying to change this pupil to "fit the school" when this may be patently impossible for him/her (at least for the time being)?'

- It is often necessary to realise that the pupil is already going through an ongoing process of adjusting to the demands made *upon him/her* in the search to preserve some sense of control and contact with peers (i.e. he/she is adapting to his/her environment not so much to 'fit in' but to survive).

- If the school demands changes in the pupil that are inconsistent with the pupil's need to have some control and contact then the pupil is not being helped.

Pupils with medical conditions

It is important to define our terms because pupils with medical conditions also fall into other categories of special need. Arguments about the benefits and problems of 'labelling' in this way are beyond the scope of this book. The important principle involved here is that the identification and assessment of SEN often involve decisions about 'priority need' or the 'dominant label'. The particular 'tag' attached to a pupil who is different in some way or has diverse needs depends upon:

- previous history and professional judgements;

- existing 'categories' or frameworks to place pupil in;

- the principles upon which the assessment is based (i.e. wholly diagnostic and individual or open and consensual);

- the provision and resources available to the LEA (responsibility to be 'efficient', e.g. cut costs if possible);

- priorities and ideologies prevalent in the system.

For example, a pupil may be regarded as 'naughty' or out of control or Level 3, say, emotional and behavioural difficulties (EBD); that is, until someone comes up with a diagnosis of attention deficit disorder (ADD). He (usually) or she then has a 'medical condition'. What difference does that make? For a start, the identification of a medical condition can have a powerful (and positive) short-term effect in the following ways:

- there is some explanation for the problem or difficulties;

- the pupil can begin to have an explanation (to himself) and stop thinking she/he is stupid or lacking;

- relief from pressure to conform and perform against the odds;

- parents can have some form of explanation to their friends and other parents.

In the short term a diagnosis of a medical condition can engender a great deal of relief and hope for remedies and positive action. In the longer term this view becomes modified when parents spend time working with diverse professionals and realise that there is rarely a 'heroic' cure for most of the medical conditions encountered (including ADD or ADHD). The reality usually involves continuous hard work, persistence to the point of obstinacy and the strength to maintain stability in the face of enormous daily stresses and pressures. A brief classification of medical conditions can be found in Cornwall (1997, p. 39), derived from Rieser and Mason (1992). More detailed information can be obtained from the growing number of support and voluntary organisations and from direct collaboration with health and medical professionals.

To achieve a balanced view of a pupil's needs and recognise the need to change the environment in some way to maintain a sensible IEP, it will be necessary to achieve a principled and balanced approach to assessment (see Institutional self-review, p. 28). Establishing principled baselines for the assessment process itself will enable a balanced approach to the IEP, increasing its chances of success. This balanced view will also necessitate an interprofessional or multi-disciplinary approach for nearly all pupils with significant disabilities, conditions or illnesses. It may be useful to consider that pupils are conscripts to a system of education that has not been designed for them as individuals. Their attainment is judged and reported by reference to age-related norms. Sometimes pupils cannot achieve excellence in a purely competitive system with narrow academic targets. However, they can always make *progress* from the baseline. Do the school and parents value and recognise this progress often made in less than conducive circumstances? Attention to and rewarding a child's own efforts to compensate for physical difficulties and gain experience through movement will increase activation. There may be other consequences in terms of relationships and access to early learning experiences. Evidence of disability is one thing. *Evidence of a positive response to it is another matter entirely.* There has been a tradition of lumping children together according to (medical) diagnosis and hence emphasising perceived problems, rather than pointing to different abilities, personal resources and individual differences.

The 1994 Code of Practice outlines, in a limited way, the nature of a pupil's learning difficulties (Table 5).

Given the right conditions and a well-adjusted learning environment a pupil with physical disabilities, for example, would not necessarily exhibit any of the above assessment criteria. Looking below the surface, on the other hand, these assessment criteria do not lead on to any rational pathways to growth and progress, nor give any clues about possible strategies or adjustments that need to be made to procedures, attitudes or the physical environment. Another problem of the statutory and procedural frameworks for all pupils – here adapted for physical disabilities and medical conditions – is the changing nature of both disabilities and medical conditions. The potential emotional difficulties proposed are not a necessary or even a permanent feature, if they exist at all. To ascribe these difficulties to an 'inability to take part' seems to ignore the fact that attitudinal, procedural or physical factors may be excluding the pupil – not just their disability or condition. So where does this leave us in terms of assessment and identification? All too often, the easy way is to concentrate upon the pupil's deficiencies or problems. How can assessment and identification become a more honest and balanced process that also recognises the opportunities and access available to, or denied to, any given pupil? For example, see Table 6.

Physical Disabilities, *resulting from illness or injury or a congenital condition, that have short- or long-term consequences*	Medical conditions *that may have an impact on a pupil's academic attainment or give rise to emotional and behavioural difficulties*
● Discrepancy between pupil's attainment and teacher's assessment	● Discrepancy between pupil's attainment and teacher's assessment
● Discrepancy between expectations of teachers, parents and specialists and attainment on the National Curriculum	● Discrepancy between expectations of teachers, parents and specialists and attainment on the National Curriculum
● Pupil requires close adult supervision and substantial adaptations ● There are significant 'self-help' difficulties or serious safety issues ● Evidence of emotional or physical stress through inability to take part . . .	● Clear evidence that the medical condition impedes or disrupts the pupil's access or participation ● Pupil's medical condition has given rise to emotional and behavioural difficulties ● There are significant and recurrent absences from school

Table 5

Assessment of individual physical or medical need	Assessment of attitudes, procedures and physical resources
● Ability to produce written work in class and complete homework	● Availability of portable word processing and training for all concerned ● Good training
● Ability to communicate effectively through alternative system and participate in class discussion	● Training in use if system (pupil and adult) is a working system ● Lesson planned and changed to include pupil (e.g. time allowed, pupil's value each other's contributions, etc.)
● Inability to participate in extra-curricular or social activities of the school	● Extra-curricular activities adjusted (place, adaptations, spaces, etc.) ● Transport arrangement reorganised or alternative found (with parents)
. . . and so on	

Table 6

It should not stop short of identifying deficiencies or difficulties and looking to external specialists or complicated technologies to solve them. In this way assessment can become part of the process of ongoing teaching and learning activities, not a dead-end process. Training and procedural changes (e.g. timetable, social events, spaces) become part of the solution. At the moment too many pupils have technology available but no one who can use it effectively – too many pupils with medical conditions suffer undue stress through trying to catch up with missed lessons. Attitudes in many schools, whether through blanket competitiveness or just plain ignorance, can lead to many pupils who are different in some way being either patronised or teased. Assessment needs to be part of or lead directly to solutions, not just a categorisation of the difficulties encountered by an individual. Assessment and identification of both individual needs and the need for significant environmental adjustments can be achieved through the curriculum and ongoing school activities. In this way assessment becomes a partnership between the teacher, the enabler or support assistant *and the pupil. They all acknowledge the context and surroundings as important and the curriculum as part of the pupil's context for learning.* It is an area where suitable adjustments can be made without sacrificing opportunity, breadth and balance. It can also serve to highlight specific areas for attitudinal, procedural and environmental changes (e.g. the recording of experiments in science or access to science facilities). This is a positive and holistic view of assessment (rather than just diagnostic or individual) that can encourage achievement and the reaching of more individual targets set out in IEPs.

In the context of school-age children and young people who are disabled or who experience prolonged periods of ill health, the concept of 'access' has to be separated from 'entitlement' and 'differentiation'. Differentiation is one way to enable participation in learning activities but it is of limited use if the student cannot get into many of the learning areas (e.g. the science laboratory) of the school or college. Access takes on additional dimensions when a physical element becomes involved but there is more to it than the purely physical. A pupil who experiences illness or a particular medical condition may suffer from tiredness or pain, such as joint pain or headaches; these may be considerably worsened by lack of attention to physical aspects of the environment.

Physical spaces for comfort for working in class/lectures; for subject specialist activities and areas; for recreation and social activities (not marginalised); for personal and hygiene needs (with dignity)

Organisation of curriculum and materials such as library or reading materials and areas available to them; speed and mode of presentation (plus catch-up time) in the classroom; availability of pre-copied materials/take away (good planning); tape recorded lessons or video material (other media); alternative ways of representing outcomes/work production; aids for communication and work production

Enrichment activities and independent learning opportunities exist where the pupil can use additional spaces around school to work/enquire; information and computer technology, materials and equipment to replace movement or relieve fatigue; facilities to join rest of group on trips; extra time to 'catch up' basic work

Learning support is well planned where assistants are not 'whisked away' arbitrarily; assistants are well trained and have empathy; medical and therapy programmes are integrated with educational activity; there is a planned process of getting equipment/aids based on regular assessments

Personal support is available but is also embedded in the social structures of the school; inclusive attitude all round (friendships, etc.); additional social spaces and activities; disability awareness (civil rights recognised); pupils are not treated differently but respected as sentient and independent personalities; systems for referral to counsellor or 'key' person on request

---

(Cornwall 1995)

Individual education planning is a cyclical process: it starts with information gathering and assessment of need; once these have been compiled it is necessary to make a judgement about the key priorities for the pupil; when this judgement has been made targets need to be set and implemented; finally, it will be necessary to review progress against the original targets. Thereafter, further assessment may be required, priorities set, further targets devised and so on.

Assessment
Phase 1

In the early stages, background information is gathered about the pupil and this could include previous records, the statement and its appendices, medical records and details obtained directly from the parents and pupil when they attend for their initial interview.

Phase 2

In this phase the pupil attends the school for an introductory period (length to be decided) during which those staff involved take part in ongoing observation and analysis. The IEP profile is used to record this information.

Judge priorities

The assessment information is compiled into a profile of the pupil's strengths and needs. A key worker may be responsible for this. A decision is then made as to the key priorities to be addressed. This decision is made at a case conference attended by a core of the staff, plus the parents and the pupil. The key areas of ability need are recorded on the IEP sheet. Some finely graded targets may need reviewing or adjusting on a daily or weekly basis, by means of interim reviews involving the key worker and lead professionals. The overall IEP is reviewed on a termly basis, in accordance with the Code of Practice. A review meeting is held, involving the key worker and a core of the staff; the parents are also invited, and the pupil included. The lead professionals report back on progress in each target area and this is recorded on the original IEP sheet. The meeting then considers modifying the overall aims and/or targets and then draws up a new IEP sheet to be implemented during the next term. Once every three terms (i.e. once a year) the review meeting is broadened to take account of the requirements of the annual review. In the year after the young person's 14th birthday the meeting would be termed the 'transition plan', involving a range of outside professionals, in accordance with the Code of Practice.

The 'individual education process' affords the opportunity for those concerned to try and understand school from the pupil's perspective so that for some of the time at least the pupil receives the individualised provision needed for progress to be made. Assessment for effective 'IEP planning' for pupils with physical disabilities or medical conditions is a skilled activity for which whole-school and individual staff development are essential. It goes beyond just looking at an individual and their particular problems to a thorough assessment of the learning environment through the attitudes, procedures and physical environment surrounding the pupil with disabilities or ill health.

Summary points

- Some pupils begin their lives or early school careers with physical disabilities or a serious medical condition, while other pupils develop disabilities or medical conditions later in their school lives.

- Assessment is important not only to establish individual needs and the need for adjustments to the learning environment and experiences of the pupil, but also to act as a way of sharing and communicating information.

- Assessment procedures for IEP planning should be housed within the whole-school procedures for curriculum and assessment.

- There is a tendency, particularly if the child has difficulties with communication, for adults to begin to take complete control of conversations and not to attempt to find a way to understand the child's (perhaps non-verbal) communications.

- Medical diagnoses are based on deficiencies, problems or impairments, whereas educational programmes are based on areas of development, growth, success and capability.

- Assessment for IEPs should be closely linked to purpose; that is, to record pupil progress, cause for concern, pupil strengths, targets and strategies.

- In order to reduce paperwork, IEP assessment information should be reported in a focused evaluative style which briefly informs the next stage of planning.

- To achieve a balanced view of a pupil's needs and recognise the need to change the environment in some way to maintain a sensible IEP, it will be necessary to achieve a principled and balanced approach to assessment.

- How can IEPs be integrated into the school's arrangements for assessing and recording the progress of all pupils (OFSTED 1996)?

- Assessment should not stop short of identifying deficiencies or difficulties and looking to external specialists or complicated technologies to solve them. In this way assessment can become part of the process of ongoing teaching and learning activities, not a dead-end process.

Individual and environmental assessment: Institutional self-review

In reading the classification, it is important to recognise that, in reality, such simplified polarisation of the issues does not exist. The issues in Table 7 (adapted from Humphreys 1992) could serve as a useful checklist for deciding on what should be included or referred to when recording and reporting.

Check this list against your own procedures:

- How many of these ideals can you achieve?
- Is there room for improvement?
- What changes could you make?

Central notions	Traditional?	Progressive?
Individual uniqueness	Group referenced and standardised	Individual and self-referenced
Different people's views	Single judgement by teacher	Multiple perspectives valued including the pupil's
Truth	Based on an assessor's bias	Based on consensus by all end users
Ownership	Evidence owned by testers	Evidence owned by pupils
Negotiation	Assessment unchallenged by the pupil	Assessment open to negotiation or dialogue
Motivation	Competitiveness allows only a few to succeed	Shared involvement allows a range of success
Context	Based on formal tests – often paper and pencil	Based on natural responses in daily context
Integration of curriculum and assessment	Assessment-led curriculum	Curriculum-led with integrated assessment
A whole view	Narrow reference based on academic achievement	Broad with reference to the whole person
Outcome	Supports selection process within the system	Supports the process of personal development

Table 7

Individual and environmental assessment: Ideas for action

Identify a pupil causing concern because of physical or medical difficulties. Locate available assessment information. Use that information to complete Table 8. What are the barriers for teachers in 'assessing for behavioural IEP planning'? What are the implications for further development?

Work in pairs and discuss answer with colleague	Fill in the following
What progress has the pupil made towards achievingexpected level (i.e. gap between 'observed' and'expected' attainment)?	What are the: ● long- and medium-term objectives; ● pupil strengths; ● draft targets and time scale for achievement; ● draft review dates?
What are the *agreed* areas of concern for this pupil?	*Agreed* targets (ensuring pupil and parent involvement and relevance of targets set)
Under what conditions does the pupil exhibit theexpected behaviour? If he is unable to exhibit thedesired behaviour the question becomes 'underwhich conditions is the frequency of theinappropriate behaviour reduced?'	● Strategies ● *Conditions* under which targets will be achieved
What is the advantage for the pupil in keeping his/her present inappropriate behaviour?	Targets (carefully designed to meet pupil needs in a more acceptable way, e.g. if pupil is exhibiting off-task behaviour in order to avoid failure the target set must be designed accordingly)
What resources (human and physical) can be harnessed towards the achievement of targets?	● *Who* is involved in IEP, i.e. roles and responsibilities, including those of pupil and parent ● Monitoring arrangements

Table 8

Information about the pupil's personal circumstances		
Family	It would be helpful to note if a parent is a step-parent.	
Others	This might include grandparents or other relatives who share responsibility for this pupil.	
Liaison	This means staff contact with parents or guardians. Please indicate daily or weekly home books, regular contact when pupil is transported to/from school, pre-arranged telephone calls, etc.	
Agencies	To include social services, etc.	
Transport	Please indicate travel arrangements to/from school and name of taxi company.	
Relevant personal history	This is a place to include other information such as change of name, unusual family circumstances, etc.	
Personal Care		
Equipment	List of special aids which are used regularly at school for this activity.	
Routines	An indication of regular times and expectations for this pupil (i.e. bath each morning).	
Preferences	Any particular likes or dislikes of this pupil during this particular routine (i.e. prefers to open doors himself . . .).	
Transfers		
By self	Please indicate situations in which the pupil needs no help to transfer, and describe method of transfer if appropriate, i.e. transfer to chair from wheelchair using table for support.	
By staff	Please indicate the number of staff needed to lift this pupil according to weight.	
Supported	Please list transfers effected by the pupil but requiring staff support, i.e. into the bath with staff assisting by lifting legs.	
Lifts	Please list situations in which the pupil is completely lifted by staff, i.e. from floor into wheelchair.	
Hoists	Please list transfers in which a hoist should be used, i.e. in/out of swimming pool.	

Table 9

Communication *This information may not be relevant for some pupils. Descriptions of communication difficulties should be agreed at case conferences and review meetings.*	
Expressive communication difficulty This would include descriptions such as motor impairment, language impairment, difficulties understanding.	
Receptive communication difficulty This would include descriptions such as sensory impairment, language impairment, difficulties understanding.	
Written communication difficulty This would include descriptions such as motor impairment, organisational difficulty.	
Augmentative strategies This would indicate the most frequently used methods of communication as an aid or alternative for any of the difficulties described above.	
Non-technical: This would include use of any aid without wires, such as signing, word board, pencil grip, eye pointing, Dycem mats, bliss or other symbol systems, etc.	
Technical This would include use of any aid with wires, such as computer, word processor, voice output communicator, switches, concept keyboard, etc.	

Table 10

Assessment check sheet

Tables 9 and 10 are examples of an *IEP's background documentation* . . . they are only examples but they illustrate the importance of environmental issues.

The background document can provide an up-to-date reference for all support staff working with an individual pupil and information during case conferences and review meetings. The key worker could be responsible for gathering information as far as is possible, and should review and update this document at least once per term.

Table 11 is intended simply to suggest ways in which significant aspects of the pupil's activity should be taken into account when assessing their needs and capabilities. It cannot be an exhaustive list because every pupil will be different and a flexible, creative approach is necessary to take account of individual circumstances. It does illustrate some of the environmental adjustments that can be made in order to make target setting a meaningful exercise (see also next chapter).

Assessment focus	Environmental adjustments
Communication	**Effective collaboration** with speech and occupational therapist – support for learning activities and access to the curriculum
Modes of communication (e.g. eye pointing, facial expression, vocalisation, gesture, words . . .)	Does the pupil have 'partners in communication' and *time* for them to focus on these responses? Are non-verbal responses interpreted or ignored? Is the pupil positioned to maximise their ability to gain attention from others?
Expressing feelings Recognising feelings Emotional vocabulary Age-appropriate expressions	Are there *opportunities* for *all to explore their feelings* (e.g. frustration, joy, achievement)? How does the pupil communicate from happy/sad through to *more complex feelings*?
Social interaction (e.g. greetings, leave taking, enquiring about, making arrangements, negotiations . . .)	Are these planned into class activity to ensure (a) that all pupils get an opportunity to experience and practise, and (b) that time and space are given for *all to be involved*?
Gaining/requesting attention Initial eye contact Vocalisation Other methods	Is sufficient time given to enable the pupil to respond or to move eyes, head, etc?
Maintaining contact and conversation Ability to maintain eye contact Asking questions Turn taking	Does the student have sufficient opportunity to ask questions – in class, out of class, etc?
Mobility, dexterity, posture	**Effective collaboration** with physiotherapist and occupational therapist – support for learning activities and access to the curriculum
Able to control head movements . . . for eye contact . . . to focus/maintain gaze . . . to communicate	Is there sufficient support when necessary without restricting the pupil's ability to scan the room (or be seen)? Is there anything worth looking at (e.g. communication partners, interesting materials in the right place)?
Maintain an upright posture Sitting on floor Sitting at table Standing – without assistance – with assistance	How stable is the pupil's seating base? – this is vital Has advice been obtained from physiotherapist or occupational therapist? Does the pupil have opportunities to change or move position – in class, different chair(s), etc?
Dexterity and manipulation Shoulder movement Arm movement Hand movement Finger movement	Does the pupil or student need an arm splint to help maintain stability? Are the pupil's posture and seating stable and comfortable to allow for hand and arm movement? Is he or she able to fix themselves with one hand while using the other, etc?
Activation and motivation in movement, mobility and position Shares/makes decisions about goals Chooses from range of activities or positions Chooses when and how to practise 'Owns' action plans Takes responsibility for self Decides who to involve Aware of stresses and strains involved	Active planning and problem solving are undertaken with the pupil involved, to develop a range of possibilities for choice Learning is related to real, everyday and personalised goals Anxiety for the pupil is reduced through successful experiences in moving Optimal preparation for physical demands enables pupil to help raise his/her own muscle potential Joint problem solving provides ownership and physical learning (as in PE curriculum)

Assessment focus	Environmental adjustments
Independence	**Independence means being able to get things done**, guiding or supervising others when necessary – not doing everything for yourself; **independence is also an attitude of mind, not just a set of skills**
Attitudes (pupil and others) Level of self-awareness Self-esteem and confidence Able to negotiate and justify Able to engage others – achieve some degree of rapport	Are there sufficient materials embedded within the school's personal and social education (PSE) or other subject curricula to discuss and develop the student's understanding and skills? Is there a facility for personal development for the pupil – that is additional and extra (e.g. mentor, key person, counsellor, etc.)?
Use of technology *Use of PC/Laptop for . . .* communication, subject work, personal organisation *Use of other technologies . . .* hearing aids/radio microphones, spectacles/visual aids	Is training available for the student and the communication partners or enablers working alongside the student?
Use of spaces, aids and adaptations *Use of classroom furniture and desk* Adjustable seating Adjustable-height table(s) Angled desk/non-slip mats Adapted writing implements Adapted writing surfaces Reading and visual materials *Use of school and play areas* Able to evacuate safely in fire Able to exit to all play areas Joins in play/social activities	Assessing the pupil's use of these materials requires careful observation of skills required and changes necessary to the materials themselves What is the goal of using this adaptation? Does it achieve that specific short-term goal? What effect is it likely to have on longer-term aims (e.g. for independence or participation)?
Use of alternative or augmentative communication systems High-technology systems Understands basic functions Understands more complex functions Uses system to its capacity Uses just in classroom Uses in a variety of places	Do these work successfully and consistently? Is sufficient time given to learning their use and to use them in daily activities?
Making decisions and choices	As above areas . . .
Participating in the curriculum	**All of the above and following factors will have an influence on this, i.e. all environmental factors such as attitudes, organisation, procedures and the physical environment**
Use of enabler, amanuensis or classroom support Use of time and timetabling Other areas?	Your environment . . .
Relationships	
Acceptance and belonging . . . Friendships and personal choices	Your environment . . .
Sensory or perceptual factors	
Organisation of work Understands schedules/timetables Check sensory functioning	
Emotional or physical stresses	It is important to have opportunities for discussion about these; some schools can do this in Circle Time activities but there need to be additional opportunities for individual contact

Table 11

Table 12 shows some of the environmental adjustments that can be made for pupils with medical conditions.

Assessment focus	Environmental adjustments . . . to attitudes, organisation and the environment
Social implications of condition	
Does the condition have any obvious physical signs that might attract negative attention?	After discussing with parents and pupil – a strategy to bring this out into the open could be adopted to avoid covert teasing, etc.
Does it hamper active participation in social events or activities (e.g. gastric tube feeding at lunch)?	Planning of additional social events or reviewing of social events to enable participation . . .
Has the pupil missed out on important social milestones and contacts?	It may not be possible to compensate fully for these but opportunities to 'plan in' experience during normal curricular/school activities could be taken . . .
Medical implications	
Is medication required? At school – at home? Regularly – intermittently?	Policy and procedures should be in place . . .
Is advice from GP/school nurse given/ recorded? How does it affect school activities, lessons and curriculum work?	Contact – pro-active planning before any problems emerge (e.g. consideration of what possible difficulties there might be . . .)
Drug therapies	
Is this going to be long-term or short-term?	Adjustments to short- and long-term targets . . . Discussion with pupil about managing and learning about the drug regime/treatments . . .
What effect does it have on the pupil's ability to concentrate? Does it make him tired?	Teacher and classroom assistants monitor pupil in class – pupil learns to recognise the effects . . . Plan additional time/space for work – suitable environment without isolating . . .
Does it mean missing chunks of work/ curriculum?	Planning with pupil and parents – deciding on priorities . . . additional work sheet, sharing the load, etc.
Emotional stresses and consequences	
Has the pupil spent time away from home, e.g. in hospital? Problems of pain, fatigue, etc?	Awareness of this and discussion with parents . . .
How have the parents coped with extra 'caring' responsibilities?	
Participating in the curriculum	
Time out of curriculum for . . . therapy sessions, doctor's appointments, out-patient treatments, hospitalisation	Multi-agency planning to minimise the academic effect and the consequent lowering of motivation and self-esteem . . . if possible Opportunity for pupil to review, with teacher, a plan to cater for missed time

Assessment focus	Environmental adjustments . . . to attitudes, organisation and the environment
Effect of drugs or treatment on . . . attentiveness or general behaviour, emotions and stability, sustaining concentration, medium-term progress, longer-term development	Planning with school nurse or medical advice and pro-active strategies for pupil to monitor this themselves Allowances made for pupil to take avoiding action when things are difficult Realistic and sympathetic appraisal of effect on academic progress and positive attitude towards problem solving with pupil and parents . . .
Health and safety factors for the pupil	
School environment – In class At play Other times (e.g. assemblies) School trips	Health and Safety policy – discussion with pupil and parents about what is safe and acceptable; encouraging full participation wherever possible

Table 12

The above tables are not exhaustive and do not cover every eventuality for every pupil but illustrate some of the attitudinal, procedural and environmental responses to individual needs for pupils who have physical disabilities or medical conditions. The IEP targets will relate to the school's curriculum as well as to individual needs (such as those above) and will take account of existing environmental factors. The setting of targets will also generate changes in attitudes, organisation and environment.

Targets, strategies and adjustments: Principles

Central to the notion of IEP planning is the principle of setting learning outcomes in advance as targets to be attained within set time periods (written as what is to be learned not how to increase the learning opportunities).

(SENJIT 1995)

This is a double-edged dilemma for teachers and SENCOs. On the one hand, it is important to devise sensible and relevant short- and medium-term targets that will promote visible progress. On the other, it is vital not to 'lose the plot' by ensuring these shorter-term targets are given meaning because they lie within a framework that has longer-term goals. The 'plot' often contains broad and grand aims such as enabling pupils to 'achieve their full potential', 'be independent as lifelong learners' and so on. These are laudable but not well-focused long-term objectives. The DfEE SENCO guide (1997) acknowledges the relevance of non-subject-based targets and describes them as 'learning targets' but it is difficult to find much educational literature that explores the notion and importance of these process skills in achieving the type of 'outcomes' that have become so central. A great deal of emphasis is now on literacy, numeracy and so-called 'behaviour' targets. This emphasis continues to penalise and exclude pupils with SEN and particularly those with physical disabilities or whose medical conditions make it difficult for them to conform to the 'literacy' demands (writing, recording or producing paper-based output) of current school-based assessment. Harris (1998), a practising SENCO, proposes the central importance of cross-curricular skills to meet the development and, by implication, individual needs of pupils while fulfilling the requirements for breadth and balance through the National Curriculum. Cross-curricular skills emphasise 'the journey', or the process by which pupils can achieve the end products of subject-based or academic targets. These include such goals as study skills and problem solving. For pupils with physical disabilities and medical conditions there are a whole range of processes, skills and adjustments that need to be made in order to make progress towards the derived outcomes.

A useful starting point might be the OFSTED criteria in 'Pupil's personal development and behaviour' (Framework, 1993, Part 1, Section 5, p. 21) and 'Attitudes, behaviour and personal development' that support and enable academic success (*OFSTED Handbook*, 10/95, 1995, Section 4.2, p. 60). These criteria support the notion that the quality of teaching, the long-term personal development of the pupil and the quality of relationships in a school are fundamental to developing positive learning attitudes in the pupil. For example, an 'assisted communicator' needs to be able to ask and answer questions in the class during lessons, not have separate dialogues with their own assistant all the time. This might require giving a little more time to answer a question or using an assistant to ask the question – guided by the pupil. It means that a pupil with diabetes or epilepsy is as challenged academically as any other pupil and given as much opportunity to persevere, sustain concentration and set targets for themselves. For pupils with physical disabilities and medical conditions, these need to be translated into:

- targets that promote and support access to the learning experiences and opportunities available to pupils in a school (these are often termed 'cross-curricular' skills);

- targets that are focused to extend an individual pupil's learning (at or just above their capabilities).

A set of pre-conditions, whether they are attitudes, skills or understanding in the physical, intellectual and social domains, are necessary for any pupil to participate in the mainstream curriculum. These pre-conditions are as various as the individuals whose 'differences' necessitate some form of special consideration in order for them to function in the current educational environment. These facts keeps rearing their messy heads in the face of attempts to set simple, neat targets at clear (and pseudo-) developmental levels. They are called by various names, such as 'cross-curricular' or 'process' skills, 'access' skills or conditions, 'bridging' curricula or, 'personal development' targets. Harris (1998) is not proposing anything radically new; he is reaffirming what teachers of pupils with special needs have understood for a long time, and he summarises the side-effects of subject-based targets:

> The attention of teachers has been fixed on outcomes on 'filling the vessel' still further, their educational leaders have failed to shift the focus towards examining how the vessel is filled.

For pupils with physical disabilities or medical conditions, there also seems to be a focus on short-term educational, therapeutic and medical targets but the long-term ramifications and aims for these pupils remain obscure and often confused. For a pupil who uses alternative and argumentative systems to communicate or who finds it impossible, for physical or medical reasons, to produce written output of the required volume at the required speed, *the process of achieving these outcomes is crucial. It raises issues of the longer-term purpose of an IEP*. Are targets set just to get a pupil through a 'sticky patch' in their education until they are 'cured' or 'rehabilitated'? Or do they need to have a longer-term purpose and aims? A pupil who becomes ill with glandular fever may go into hospital for a time and then perhaps miss 3 or 4 months of school. He or she will need support and planning just as much as a pupil with long-term epilepsy or diabetes. The difference lies in the nature of the targets and their links to longer-term needs. It is assumed that the pupil with glandular fever will, at some point, be able to relinquish the support and planning (say, when he or she has 'caught up') – although this may not always be the case. It is also assumed that a pupil with cerebral palsy will always need a significant level of support, which also may not be the case, once certain basic needs and conditions have been met. The situation is complex and, as always, depends upon problem solving, flexibility and individual situations or circumstances. Setting targets, particularly for pupils with physical disabilities or medical conditions, needs a firm grasp of a complex situation, not a limited focus on 'What's wrong with the pupil? Let's put it right.'

The Code of Practice (1994) specifies limited examples of some of the means of gaining access to educational activities (e.g. technology, word processors, switch input, space in the classroom, maintenance of equipment and access to independent learning and the physical environment). Similarly, for pupils with medical conditions the exemplified educational provision is limited to involving health and medical services, collaboration, form filling and developing a 'consistent approach to managing the child's education'. There is little indication of the range of cross-curricular and process skills needed, which leaves us all with the problem of defining these and somehow 'blending' them with the ever-present subject-based attainments. In analysing target setting, we are attempting to provide examples of the ways in which these 'process' skills and 'access' skills can enhance the process of target setting without losing sight of the broad curriculum and the longer-term aims for the pupil.

It now remains to identify a range of examples and a framework for analysing and developing cross-curricular or process skills that are relevant to pupils with physical disabilities and medical conditions. It is also important that the generation of individual targets takes place in a learning environment and within a school ethos and approach in which *significant adjustments have been made to include these pupils and to ensure equality of opportunity*. While schools have tackled the design of formats and the application of IEPs, there is now a need to further develop effective procedures for monitoring and evaluating the *educational* value for individual pupils. There is little doubt that documentation is largely in place but procedures to review and ensure that progress is taking place for individuals are still very much in development.

A great many of the problems for pupils with disabilities stem from the *attitudes and behaviour of others and bureaucratic or disabling traditions, environments and procedures*. In this context their individual targets become more and more limited and meaningless, not extending a pupil because they are limited by their environment and by the views of those around them. Perhaps, more than any other form of SEN, this group of students is likely to be penalised by lack of, or insufficient access to, specific resources, adaptations or creative use of simple and complex technological solutions. For example, effective communication (oral and literal) is not just a necessity to fulfil the requirements of the English curriculum but necessary for all curriculum areas and for life in general.

Can school intervention and IEPs make a difference or are the problems too large and external to the classroom to enable change to take place? If so-called 'standards' are only referenced against external criteria, such as General Certificate of Secondary Education (GCSE) and Standard Assessment Tests (SAT) results, then it is difficult to reconcile the two key themes of the Green Paper 'Excellence for all children...' (DfEE 1998), namely raising standards and including pupils. What standards are we talking about and who sets them? For what purpose are they set? The pursuit of excellence and the very definition of the term mean that many will not achieve 'excellence' because, if we all achieve it, it becomes the 'average'. The problems also stem from the influences and attitudes of society as a whole, which have become focused on academic achievement as the main purpose of schooling, typified by exam results and academic accreditation. Society in general is only just becoming aware of the rights of disabled people, now partially encapsulated in the 1997 Disability Discrimination Act.

> Schools do not work in a vacuum, nor do staff work in a climate unaffected by the larger, different worlds within which we and our pupils live.
>
> (McGuinness 1994)

It is important to be clear about the problems for the school or an individual teacher. There may be factors inherent in the way the school is run or there may be events in a pupil's life at school, such as bullying or harassment, that contribute to disaffection or passivity. In any situation where pupils with physical disabilities or medical conditions are experiencing difficulties in learning or accessing the curriculum or where there are problems for a school in making 'reasonable adjustments', it is important to consider the factors that:

- teachers can influence directly;
- require a whole-school approach;
- require support from outside the school;
- are determined completely outside schools altogether.

This has important ramifications for the development and use of IEPs. It is tempting to believe that teachers can have no influence over social or medical factors that emanate from sources beyond school. This is not so. Carefully planned IEPs and sensitively executed intervention in a classroom may not change the world outside or alter the 'natural biological diversity' (Reindal 1995) of the individuals in a class. However, they may have considerable impact upon the 'community' of the classroom as well as on an individual pupil's effort, will to learn, participation, enjoyment of education and, in the end, attainment at school.

Adopting a 'socially responsible' attitude does not mean ignoring the factors that are within the child, or are immediately impacting on the way they function in school or the way they see themselves generally. You could say that these are also affected by family life and by the school but, for the purposes of problem solving effectively through the formulation of an IEP, we need to separate out the effects of the condition from the environmental (physical and social) influences and their sources as a first step. We must not forget then that *teachers and other adults who work directly with children experiencing disabilities or medical conditions are a major part of the solution to their difficulties*. The interactive and transactional nature of these types of problems means that relationships are fundamental to an educational or social perspective as opposed to a medical one.

Purpose of targets

The purpose of targets goes beyond their effect on an individual pupil. They:

- provide a focus for *coordinated educational effort* because everyone involved shares a common goal;
- strengthen the links between policy, planning and provision;
- provide a means for assessing the effectiveness of provision;
- support staff development in relation to SEN;
- provide realistic challenges;
- provide more rigorous criteria for the reporting of progress;
- establish agreed priorities of need.

Rationale

Target writing assumes that:

- what is learned can be broken down into its constituent parts;
- these parts can be described as distinct targets;
- these parts can be set out as a linear sequence;
- the final desired learning outcome can be achieved by meeting each sub-target in the sequence;
- methods of teaching can be identified from these targets.

Targets arise from the assessment of pupil progress within the curriculum and their individual profile of strengths and weaknesses. The *educational effectiveness* of targets rests on their design and selection as well as the shared belief of those involved that they are realistic and worthwhile. The setting of targets can provide a focus for the collaborative educational effort and may involve parents and learners in target setting. Furthermore, planning to achieve targets can direct attention to the efficient use of resources and the direct linking of teaching to learning outcomes. The achievement of targets can be a measure of the effectiveness of IEPs and, therefore, of the school's SEN provision. It is important to remember, however, that targets do not exist independently. Setting them does not in itself achieve anything; nor does it necessarily result in effective teaching. There are many potential *pitfalls in writing targets* and these are dealt with extensively in Tod *et al.* (1998).

The currently favoured model is to provide teachers with guidance on how to write targets and then to provide them with lists of targets linked to categories of need. This method could be useful as a way of improving teacher competence in planning for SEN teaching, provided the aim is not simply to achieve 'technical competence' so that the IEP procedure can continue to be seen to be operational. The design and selection of educationally relevant targets require more than technical competence. They require at the very least a knowledge and understanding of individual differences in a pupil's condition and circumstances, and an understanding of the substantive issues surrounding teaching approaches that reduce curriculum complexity and increase access for the pupils with phyiscal disabilities or medical conditions.

A key feature of effective school policies on special needs were: Practical Strategies for the identification and assessment of pupils' short-, medium- and long-term difficulties, with clear expectations and advice for staff on writing IEPs.

(OFSTED 1996)

Types of targets

It might be useful to provide teachers with a taxonomy of targets. These could fall into three categories:

- *direct linkage:* target = learning outcome;

- *flexible linkage:* target = range of possible learning outcomes;

- *indirect linkage:* target = an outcome which can be recognised but not prescribed.

Alternatively, targets might be classified as:

- 'access' targets;

- 'process' targets;

- 'response' targets;

- 'curriculum' targets;

- 'personal development' targets' etc.

Table 13 shows how targets can be useful in different ways, for example, for a pupil who uses a wheelchair to get about and an amanuensis for recording and who is an assisted communicator.

Working with an amanuensis or an enabler does not mean a lack of independence. It is the management and use of those resources (including the human element) that define independence for a pupil with physical disabilities. It is no use defining independence as a struggle to be like everyone else or to 'do it yourself' all the time. This is not a satisfactory target for many disabled pupils and students. Judgements about lack of effort, laziness or 'manipulation' do not come into it. There is simply an aim to achieve educationally, whatever the means. If the support is available, it must be used efficiently. If it is not available, then creative means have to be found. Changing the actual target means under-achievement by the pupil or student – so the type of activity or the nature of the task needs to be changed.

	Direct linkage target = single or discrete learning outcome(s)	Flexible linkage target = range of possible learning outcomes	Indirect linkage target = outcome can be recognised but not prescribed
Access	Is able to look at teacher or establish an appropriate position for focusing on class activities during the lesson	Will make it known to the teacher if he/she does not understand (either by sign or via enabler)	Maintains and perseveres at the task given; aware of and able to communicate fatigue and low concentration levels
Process	Will listen to and indicate understanding of instructions with yes/no, if appropriate (or via communication system)	Will record information in a 'notebook' (using amanuensis) or on appropriate technology – when teacher is giving instructions	Will join in class discussions and will indicate (via communicator or enabler) any lack of opportunity
Response	Will indicate tools or resources needed for this task (with amanuensis or enabler)	Will make a brief (oral/visual) plan before starting and check it through with enabler/teacher	Will organise self (and enabler or technology) so as to be able to respond to tasks/activities
Curriculum	Will identify and mark six principal cities on a map of England, or a local place of interest on an Ordnance Survey map	Will make a map and some detailed plans of a real place – one of the principal cities or local places of interest	Will enjoy creating a radio travelogue and commentary to accompany the map
Personal development (e.g. self-esteem)	Will evaluate the effectiveness of note taking and recording procedures in that lesson with teacher or enabler	Will discuss with enabler the degree of support required to complete this kind of task – assert independent evaluation of help	Will maintain some control over organisation of their work and develop independence skills and confidence

Table 13

A similar outline for a pupil with a medical condition might look something like Table 14. In this case the focus is on remaining as independent as possible in learning, taking responsibility but at the same time making (and asking for) adjustments or alternative plans. The pupil or student in this case is adjusting to the restrictions imposed by their condition and expecting and organising others to help them prioritise their work.

In summary

- Target setting is a challenging task for teachers due to the fact that 'cause for concern' from which targets are generated is subject to the effects of environmental changes.

- Target achievement may also be unstable – due not to IEP inconsistencies but to the effects of out-of-school factors.

- One key principle behind target setting is the need to *'measure'* progress. It is reasonable to deal with 'observable' outcomes, which is why physical disability and medical condition IEPs tend to be limited to such things as 'will communicate hello' or 'dress independently'. For some pupils there is a need to address more complex targets or personal goals.

- Teachers may have identified a cause for concern but feel that they should target something else just because it can be written as an observable, achievable target. Generating targets does become quicker with experience and teachers have made considerable progress in developing skills in SMART target writing.

- Schools should not judge targets just in terms of 'goodness of fit' with Code of Practice and LEA requirements for accountability, but also in terms of compatibility with the medium- and long-term aims for meeting the physical or medical and learning needs of the pupil.

- While the accountability function of IEPs cannot be ignored it should not take precedence over the educational function. For this reason a 'balanced diet' of targets for pupils (i.e. both individual and curricular) is recommended.

- Finally, setting targets can be highly inaccurate without due consideration of the environmental (physical and social) factors at work and will not reflect pupils' true academic level or be appropriate to their progress in learning.

	Target = direct (learning outcome = target)	Target = flexible linkage (possible learning outcomes)	Indirect linkage (outcome recognised but not prescribed)
Access	Is able to maintain appropriate 'focus' on selected lessons and select priorities for attendance	Will make it known to the teacher if he/she has missed specific areas of study and would like additional material	Aware of and able to communicate pain or discomfort
Process	Will listen to and indicate understanding of instructions/scheme of work and arrange or ask for flexible or additional input, as necessary/possible	Will record task information (by whatever means) when teacher is giving instructions (or ask for alternative or prepared worksheets)	Will join in class discussions when possible but has an alternative plan for dealing with/coping with additional demands
Response	Will indicate this or alternative task if this one is unrealistic (in terms of time or level)	Will complete work task or agree later date for completion with teacher; will be able to plan realistic schedule for work completion	Will organise self, in terms of time allocation, with alternative work as agreed and appropriate
Curriculum	Will identify and mark six principal cities on a map of England	Will make maps and plans of a real place in the local area	Will enjoy reading about and identifying local places of interest on the map
Personal Development (e.g. self-esteem)	Will draw a personal timetable of work linked to the school timetable	Will develop skills and an understanding of negotiation skills – to plan work schedules that are achievable	Will develop the confidence to negotiate current priorities successfully and appropriately

Table 14

Targets, strategies and adjustments: Institutional self-review

Target setting

Examine the targets contained within the school's IEPs for pupils with physical disabilities or medical conditions (Table 15).

Question – pupils with physical disabilities or medical conditions	Implications for school development	Action
● What kinds of outcomes are expected in response to target setting? Are they reasonable and do they really measure what the pupil knows and can do?		
● Are targets set compatible with medium- and long-term aims for the pupil concerned?		
● Are targets set with due regard for environmental factors and adjustments to the physical and learning environment?		
● Do targets translate into educationally relevant outcomes? Who is mainly responsible for target setting (e.g. SENCO, pastoral care, class teacher or subject teacher)?		
● Have pupils been involved in their own target setting (including assisted communicators)?		
● Are the targets set clear and are the environmental adjustments, technological or other aids or particular conditions necessary also clear, to all concerned?		
● Are targets accompanied by 'how achievement of targets will be judged' and by a clear statement of 'under what conditions'?		
● Does target progression reflect the need of pupils to practise and generalise new skills and understanding in a range of settings?		
● Do they address the 'different or extra' provision needed for pupils concerned?		
● Do they avoid isolating and excluding the pupils concerned by too much 1:1 or segregate by working with adults only?		

Table 15

The 10 key strategies

The following strategies provide a summary of ways in which learning activities, lessons (and plans) and subject work could be made more accessible to pupils (Blamires 1997), with notes and adaptations for pupils with physical disabilities or medical conditions).

Strategy 1:

Clarity of what is expected

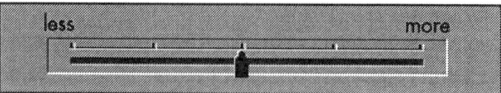

Is the equal opportunities policy of the school made explicit through procedures and attitudes and is it applied with explanation and understanding? Does the learner know what the task is, how much they are expected to do, when they are finished and what they have to do next? Does the learner know the *implicit* routines of the school and class and have reasonable adjustments been made? Are areas with specific functions accessible? Does the learner know 'the way we do things here' and why? Does the learner have a personal timetable so they know where they are in the day and during the week and does it enable them to participate in educational and social activities?

Strategy 2:

Predictability/novelty

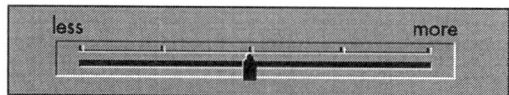

Is the day or lesson structured to allow for different rates of work? Are there sufficient opportunities for a pupil or student to choose an alternative activity, should fatigue set in (or change mode of activity)? Would different activities, groupings and settings make the basic activity more achievable or interesting?

Strategy 3:

Affirmation/criticism

Are there opportunities to reward the real effort of an individual? Does the way the reward is given take account of the need for privacy (e.g. a pupil may not want to appear 'slow' in comparison with others) or diplomacy (others may have worked hard too) with peers? Does the teacher's/adult's response affirm the effort, in terms of personal cost, and is this related to personal achievement goals, too? Is there an opportunity for the pupil/student to review their own way of going about the task(s) – for efficiency, time, economy of effort, etc? Are opportunities to affirm the pupil's participation in the curriculum and regular class activities taken?

Strategy 4:

Interaction/group work

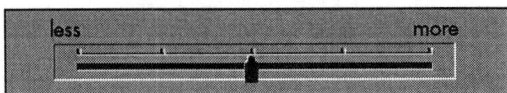

Is flexible grouping in operation that avoids the negative effect of sink groups or exclusion and isolation from any group because of aids or adaptations? Are learners able to work by themselves if required or seek the appropriate support from peers? Are learners encouraged to learn through group discussion and activity? Is the child involved and able to participate by dint of position, differentiation and use? If aids (including wheelchairs) are used, are the adults aware of the potentially isolating nature of these (e.g. different heights, etc.)? Are peers able to work with assisted communicators who may be using alternative means to communicate?

Strategy 5:

Available time for tasks (workload)

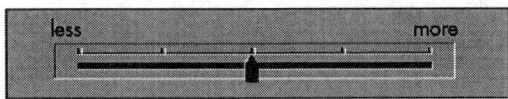

Is the workload appropriate for the learner? Has he/she too much or too little to do? Is the amount of time available for tasks including homework enough? Could the learner increase their work rate via the use of a laptop or computer? Are the available adaptations and aids organised effectively so as not to waste any time in learning or activity? Has the availability of time – to catch up, to get organised, to review methods and to use additional aids or technology – been planned for?

Strategy 6:

Negotiation/conflict (choice)

Does the learner have choice? Is he/she supported to develop independent learning and social skills? Are there opportunities for 'real' negotiation so that passivity can be avoided? Is there a flexible and fair system of evaluation and discussion available to encourage problem solving and independent learning? Is the learner who has, for example, been away from school for a significant period, able to feel that he/she can plan her work programme with the teacher?

Strategy 7:

Level of work (complexity)

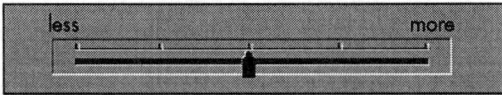

Is the work easy enough for the learner to do? Could it be broken down into smaller constituent tasks? On the other hand, does it set enough challenges? Are links made with other areas? Is the use of aids or technology or negotiated timetables well organised enough to enable the learner to work at her own level of academic potential?

Strategy 8:

Modality

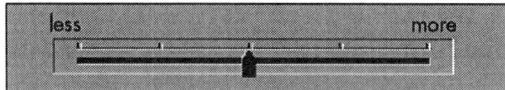

Are tasks set, undertaken and presented just using spoken language? Can multi-sensory approaches be applied and the preferred modality of the learner be emphasised? Can worksheets and additional information be prepared beforehand in an oral activity – so the pupil with a disability can concentrate on content rather than the process of note taking? Do some activities lend themselves to the abilities of a pupil with a disability – so they can experience some success (e.g. a seated game or activities using IT)? Are teacher input and pupil output being recorded in a variety of ways?

Strategy 9:

Reading demand

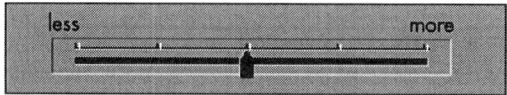

Is the reading demanded from the tasks appropriate? Is the readability level too difficult? Is the page layout of materials cluttered or too busy? Do key words need to be taught? Is there too much reading necessary for the task – could it be displayed differently? Does the pupil have access to literary sources – books and stories, for example – in alternative forms (e.g. book tapes that a pupil does not have to handle so much or turn pages)? Is sufficient time being given to read and understand in other subject lessons?

Strategy 10:

Attention (given or expected)

Does the child require extra monitoring and support by the teacher or support staff in order to be able to respond to expectations? Can self-help skills and independence be developed through organisation and negotiation? Do the adults respond to the learner's assessment of how much help they need – particularly physically or for communication? Is there a planned approach to the degree of support (or hands off strategies) given to any one pupil? How much attention from support staff or an enabler does a pupil need? Are the skills of managing the help or negotiating alternative timetables catered for in planning the IEP?

Targets, strategies and adjustments: Ideas for action

Inclusive strategies in the classroom that provide a base for individual target setting

- Targets should always be linked to long-term aims for pupil's personal and educational development.

- Aims, targets and strategies emerge out of a process of assessment of progress.

- They should not be 'taken off the shelf' but need to be adapted to meet the needs of the individual.

- 'New' skills or environmental adjustments need to be developed through the context of pupils' everyday activity – i.e. *embedded* – at school; that is, through curriculum and extra-curricular activity.

- Progress made should be charted from baseline (i.e. relative), not against norms for same-age peers (i.e. absolute).

Suggestions for/examples of inclusive strategies . . .	Leading to potential individual targets . . .
For the pupil who uses a wheelchair, they are seated where there is no unpredictable movement behind.	Pupil expresses an opinion when involved in decisions about where they should sit.
For pupils with additional auditory and/or visual problems the pupil should be seated at the front of the classroom or as near to the teacher and blackboard as possible, not at an angle.	Pupil is able to signal or point out to the teacher or other adult/enabler when he or she cannot see or hear properly.
The pupil should have his own personal designated space around him.	Keeping only necessary items on the desktop. If using small objects such as counters, put them in a pot. A clipboard or a bulldog clip to keep papers together.
Observe a pupil's strengths and encourage any pupil or student with a disability to organise a group activity in which they can show these strengths. The strengths may be academically related or creative (e.g. mime using the hands only) or they may have to do with out of school activities. Self-esteem is so important (see pp. 20–35).	Will become more aware of his/her own strengths and capabilities.
Teachers should be ready for *specialised and high-technology equipment* to be part of the classroom environment and be aware of signs that it is not working properly. They should be aware of referral systems for technical support and technical support should be available. This requires forward planning rather than reaction to breakdowns.	Do not assume knowledge of IT by the pupil if he or she is disabled and uses, for example, a communicator. Pupil will learn to assess own abilities and levels with IT. Pupil will develop their skills at evaluating the effectiveness and efficiency of technology/aids for their purposes – and be able to express this evaluation.

Suggestions for/examples of inclusive strategies . . .	Leading to potential individual targets . . .
Advice on classroom management should be at hand – for instance on the durability and suitability of certain furniture since some items are less stable, adaptable or appropriate. The teacher may need advice on adaptations to help the pupil manage books, pencils and other materials.	Pupil contributes by formulating their own opinions of (or communicating in a basic way – depending upon age and development) the suitability, comfort and efficiency of aids or adaptations.
Talking books can aid learning for pupils who are physically exhausted by traditional methods of reading.	Pupil will enjoy listening to stories and access literature which would otherwise be difficult because of problems physically handling the book(s).
Written work – try different grips or different thicknesses of pen shaft; wrap the pencil in an elastic band or textured material; this may help relax grip and control pressure. Try using thicker paper. Use graph paper for maths.	Pupil expresses opinions about the suitability of different grips, positions, sizes, etc.
Weighting the pupil's pencil box or other containers that he uses so that the contents do not get knocked over so easily.	Pupil decides best position for pencil box or other containers, papers, etc. – on the desk.
Pupils and students with disabilities may expend more energy for less result than a non-disabled student, thus reducing the length of time they can work at any one time, within the full school day. The class *teacher needs to be alert to signs of fatigue*, to provide opportunities for rest and reduce work volume where necessary.	Pupil develops an ability to monitor his/her own level of fatigue and motivation. This goes with building up stamina and perseverance but being able to express clearly when it is becoming counter-productive. Encouragement to build up stamina should be given, as it is with all children.
Help pupil identify steps needed to begin and finish the task. You may need to write down the steps or at least get the pupil to repeat directions.	Pupil plans, with enabler, any additional help at the start of an activity (or the school day). Also plans what assistance is needed to complete/ record task at the end (with enabler, as appropriate).
Set short pieces of work so that the pupil can achieve success in completing a task (increasing motivation).	Pupil self-monitors and moves on to further planned tasks – as planned, without waiting.
Teachers should remember that *writing aids are not necessarily there to increase speed*, but are useful for pupils for whom writing is difficult or who need to conserve energy.	Pupil will negotiate extra time to complete tasks when necessary. Also negotiate acceptable ways to cut down the amount of writing without losing the effect or meaning of the activity/writing/task.
Establish the length of time required for the pupil to complete a task and structure the task so that it may be completed within that time. Mark the pupil's desk with left and right markers. Mark the paper to know where to start and stop.	Pupil will move from very structured tasks to begin with to longer, more complex and less structured tasks – developing confidence and independence in learning along the way.
Help the pupil physically to move through the action.	Pupil will discuss and express or indicate clearly just how much help is needed (e.g. the amount of physical support) with any given action.
Give one direction at a time. Use short, simple, one-concept phrases to give directions. You may have to repeat verbal directions slowly, firmly and clearly for all children. Give a visual demonstration if possible. Ensure the pupil can see your face when giving instructions. Do not give instructions while the pupil is engaged in an activity.	Pupils are being encouraged to focus their attention on the tasks/instructions being given. Pupils will learn to pay attention when instructions are given carefully and clearly. Pupil will indicate effectively when instructions are not understood.
Where teaching techniques are good, they will not need to be changed for pupils with disabilities but teachers will need to be flexible as to volume (but not quality) of work and the way it is produced. There may be a need to *differentiate work appropriately*.	Pupils will (at certain ages and developmental levels) learn to negotiate priorities with the teacher/enabler. At younger ages pupils will learn to recognise their own strengths and needs and adjust their responses accordingly.

Suggestions for/examples of inclusive strategies ...	Leading to potential individual targets ...
If pupils have *difficulties with coordination* be prepared to tape paper to the desk or provide large pencils. Similarly, a slant board, providing a correctly angled surface, is useful for pupils who find horizontal surfaces impossible or difficult to work on. It is important that desktop materials are manageable and do not slide around. One way to solve this is to have them on a computer screen, where they are manageable.	Pupils, early on, will learn to use a variety of media, technology and aids to achieve their objectives. As they get older, they will learn to pay attention to the process of getting organised (and organising others, e.g. their enabler) to be able to meet academic work requirements.
Tag board or paper strips clipped to a board can be invaluable aids as place keepers for pupils with erratic head or hand movements. *Helping the pupil to keep his/her place, or presenting material in small segments,* can often make the difference between independent *learning* and time-consuming one-to-one tutoring.	Pupil will learn to indicate/communicate when he or she has completed a piece of work and/or is moving on to the next piece – or is ready to move on.
If writing or *recording work ideas* is particularly difficult then a helper, amanuensis, laptop, concept keyboard or tape recorder can be used during tests. The *handling of books and materials* may be very difficult for some physically disabled pupils and can consume much energy. A slant board or book holder can be of great benefit; many kinds are commercially available.	Pupil will learn to evaluate different ways of recording their work – for time, efficiency, clarity, finished product, etc.; also to indicate how these aids are best used (e.g. position, etc.). Will evaluate the efficiency of the aids in terms of the amount of output they can generate with given effort (and the quality of that output).
Inform the pupil if classroom routine is to be changed so that they are prepared. Work routines should not be disrupted regularly by withdrawal of support staff, without planning and advance warning for the pupil. It has longer-term disruptive consequences.	Pupil establishes and maintains a class routine for themselves but able to adapt this (with enabler) when necessary.
Pupils with disabilities are able and *entitled to take part in physical education*. A programme may require specialist help to begin with. Where specific medical conditions exist, advice should be sought.	Pupil evaluates their own abilities and skills in relation to the PE curriculum – at whatever level they can function. Pupil develops confidence in movement (however limited it may be). Pupil evaluates their own abilities and skills in relation to the PE curriculum – at whatever level they can function. Pupil develops confidence in movement (however limited it may be). Evaluates their own targets and develops alternative targets as appropriate.
Physical education is also about sportsmanship and cooperation. Pupils with disabilities may use muscles with abnormal tone to perform necessary tasks. All available adaptive methods and/or aids must be used in order to increase independence and efficiency of working.	Pupil will learn about cooperation and sportsmanship by joining in with activities in some active capacity (not on sidelines). Pupil (at certain ages) recognises common ground with physiotherapy activities and adapts accordingly.
Teachers must be confident about specific procedures and able to deal with some of the consequences of asthma, epilepsy or diabetes in case of emergencies (e.g. to cope with a seizure, to have sugar available). Managing continence is also an important and sensitive area. Once procedures have been worked out and as confidence increases, these events cease to be emergencies and become part of the daily management of the pupil's health.	Pupil expresses clear views about dignity and privacy in personal hygiene matters. Pupil takes part in discussion, whenever possible, about procedures (medical, therapeutic or other health) and takes some responsibility for their actions (appropriate to understanding, age, etc.). Young pupils begin to develop expectations about their personal requirements and about privacy and dignity.

Suggestions for/examples of inclusive strategies . . .	Leading to potential individual targets . . .
Classmates can be a tremendous source of help and support without requiring this formally. As part of friendship they will become familiar with the pupil's practical requirements. This can also be facilitated through general disability awareness work and by sensitively handled discussions in groups or with the class as a whole. Consider safety aspects carefully (e.g. lifts).	Can develop a real understanding of the nature of their conditions or disability. With preparation they are able to discuss it and talk about it with peers in planned situations (in a proper supportive atmosphere). They are able to express practical day-to-day requirements and their expectations of those that help – their needs and the needs of the group, too.
Important notices and posters must be within easy sight, perhaps placed lower than normally, particularly if the pupil is a wheelchair user. Teachers have noticed the degree of independence this gives pupils, enhancing feelings of being part of the class.	Pupil will participate in the social life of the class and school. Pupil is interested in social events and information. Younger pupils develop social skills and friendship – enhancing self-esteem and confidence.
The classroom should be organised in such a way that the pupil's *social, cultural and emotional development*, as well as academic progress, are encouraged as much as possible. Very good results have been achieved by discussing the problem with the class. Such discussions reinforce pupils' awareness of the need for tidiness, for instance pushing in chairs when not in use or not leaving bags or books blocking aisles, so as to allow freedom of movement for a wheelchair or a pupil with walking aids.	Pupil understands what adjustments are being made (physically and socially) in the classroom and can contribute to these. Will develop understanding of group functioning and will express wishes and needs in that forum – at appropriate age and developmental levels.
All pupils should have an *equal chance to take part in the school's extra-curricular activities*. Advance planning may be necessary, particularly if the pupil is taken to school by taxi. The fact that some pupils do have to come to school by taxi should not prevent pupils taking part in extra-curricular activities if at all possible.	Pupil will develop expectations for involvement in school, community and social activities along with other children. Pupil will develop increasing expectations for participation in community life outside school.
Different standards of behaviour or work from disabled pupils are not necessary. They should be expected to participate in school rules with their classmates. Pupils should be mobile, with or without aids, so they can be asked to undertake tasks outside the classroom or run errands as often as other pupils.	Pupil will learn that relationships are based on mutual respect and understanding (along with all pupils). Pupil expects respect and will, in turn, learn to contribute to and participate in class or group – along with others.
Encourage the pupil to talk about their problems and frustrations so as to avoid unnecessary tension and stress. Opportunities to talk through difficulties should be afforded and not left to chance. A good pastoral system can achieve this, along with a 'key worker'.	Pupil learns to monitor both the internal (e.g. pain, fatigue, discomfort) effects of the disability or condition *and* the external effects (e.g. expectations, seating . . .) and to express this clearly. Pupils learn to express their feelings about their abilities and difficulties (e.g. communication, etc.) in an appropriate forum.

The aim of this development activity is to consider the fact that inclusive strategies may be used to generate IEP targets for pupils with physical disabilities or medical conditions.

Coordination and monitoring: Principles

This chapter is concerned with the various facets of leadership, coordination and management that make for effective inclusion of pupils with disabilities, but also with *improvement of quality of life and education for all pupils.* Confronting the issues for pupils with disabilities more often than not offers an invaluable opportunity *to examine the quality of education generally in a school.* Good-quality education means maximum achievable consistency throughout a child's or young person's educational experience. This is not to be confused with uniformity or a reduction to a minimum, arbitrary or limited view of 'standards'. A child or young person who cannot participate fully in their local community will often have equal difficulty accessing education and its potential benefits. Leadership, management, coordination and teamwork are essential components in providing good-quality education and quality of life for all pupils and students, but particularly for this group.

The task of coordinating the physical and social environment, as well as the individual needs of the pupil (see pp. 11–35), is a challenge to the managerial and creative skills of the SENCO. To then plan and coordinate the enactment and regular review of the IEP and its targets also requires well-developed collaborative and advisory skills. This section of the book considers the complex process and also includes some frameworks to assist the SENCO in the process of *monitoring not just the IEPs themselves but the process by which they are planned, implemented and evaluated.*

Individual needs may have arisen from a range of factors – those within the individual (e.g. medical or illness), their family or community context, the school curriculum and procedures, the school environment (physical and social), their socio-economic environment or a combination of these. The IEP procedure was developed in recognition of the fact that some pupils with SEN needed to have educational effort clearly focused towards meeting a *few clearly defined targets irrespective of the complexities of attributed causation.* The IEP was designed to be additional to and not instead of other SEN provision provided by the school.

> At the core of the Code's endorsement of the IEP lies a simple idea: if an institution or group of people gather their efforts round one or more straightforward objectives and review, after a specified time, whether these objectives have been achieved the desired change is more likely to take place.
>
> (SCAA 1996)

Pupils with physical disabilities or medical conditions often have a range of additional agencies involved due to the nature of their difficulties. For example, a pupil who becomes ill or has, say, a road traffic accident and is absent from school for some time will require some intervention of a medical nature and, most likely, from the hospital school services. A pupil with cerebral palsy may require physiotherapy in order to learn to manage their physical movement and speech therapy to support the development of effective communication. *The teacher, with support from assistants, enablers and the SENCO, is still responsible* for supervising these aspects of a pupil's progress. The process of planning, implementing and evaluating is a circular one. That is, it is an on-going one – a cycle of events that repeats itself in the process of establishing and maintaining an effective IEP. There may come a time when, for example, a pupil has been ill for a period of time but then recovers and has not been ill for between 18 months and two years. By this time it should be possible for the pupil to be monitored again by the regular pastoral activities of the school. Generally speaking *the maintenance of the IEP is important, so that it changes as the pupil grows, develops and achieves targets set*. It must not remain static. If it does, then the pupil is not making progress and the targets need changing or the pupil has made progress but it has not been recognised – again the targets need changing.

An IEP is a plan of action for the professionals and staff working with that pupil and a plan for the pupil himself or herself (and sometimes for the parents, too). The successful implementation of that plan is brought about by the skill of the SENCO, and with support from school management, flexibility and commitment from all. Monitoring a pupil's progress, particularly the medium-term progress, through this plan, requires equal levels of commitment, collaboration and thought to make it effective. The pupil's attitudes and personal development, increased access through therapy and other programmes and their opportunity to participate fully in the curriculum play an important role in the development of effective IEPs. These are the responsibility of *all members of staff with support from the SENCO*; this too should be monitored.

The SENCO should be a member of the school management team and have time allocated away from classroom teaching, in order to facilitate important whole-school innovations and responses, particularly for pupils experiencing physical disabilities and medical conditions. In this part of the book the role and skills of a SENCO are considered alongside the relationship between colleagues working together to bring IEPs to fruition for the benefit of pupils. The Code of Practice (1994) outlines in brief the major areas that the SENCO is responsible for in the school. It is a starting point for monitoring consistency and cohesion in the school's approach to pupils experiencing physical disabilities and medical conditions, through the IEPs. It is a responsible and occasionally insecure role within a school, depending on the relationship between the SENCO, the staff and the school management team.

Senior management has a vital role in providing high-quality leadership within schools, and in managing effectively a range of tasks (including timetabling, providing support for staff and liaising with parents, governors, the LEA, etc.) that influence the attitudes, organisation and physical environment within schools. A *professional approach to every child* has to do with creating a positive, energetic and inclusive atmosphere in the classroom. A great deal can be achieved when pupils who have different needs begin to be looked upon as an integral part of the class, not as a professional problem that causes disruption or 'needs to be dealt with . . .'. When such a pupil, who may have physical disabilities or medical conditions, is accepted as part of the solution to any difficulties that may arise, then significant progress is usually made.

This does not mean, for example, that a school can completely eliminate the functional disadvantages experienced by pupils with physical disabilities and medical conditions, but a child with effective IEP arrangements may do better academically and will feel more valued than a child attending a school with ineffective or non-existent arrangements. *Schools do influence the opportunities, the standard of work and the life chances of a child.* To a significant degree, the success of the SENCO depends upon some fundamental conditions being in place.

Managing the physical and social environment

The senior management team will need to consider the school's internal management structure to take account of pupils with physical disabilities. *Clear lines of responsibility should be in place and understood by all staff,* before pupils with disabilities or medical conditions are admitted. In particular, the roles to be played by guidance and learning support staff, and the relationship between each, need to be clearly defined. It will prove beneficial to identify a key person or 'contact' teacher for each pupil with a physical disability. The 'contact' teacher's relationships with guidance and/or learning support departments will need to be defined, as will the method of reporting back on pupil progress to the senior management team or year tutors. However, the process of putting in place an effective management structure – that is, one that receives commitment and cooperation – is not simple. It is here that varying attitudes towards pupils and students with disabilities or medical conditions may be encountered.

Experience has shown that it is good practice to engage in broad discussion before launching into specific changes that may be sabotaged by hidden agendas. This can be a difficult and sometimes painful experience but it is fundamental to making further progress. Attitudes are vital in achieving commitment and in sharing views. It is important at this point that people are able to discuss their views openly in order to achieve consensus. It is also important that disapproval of a diversity of views is replaced by information giving and negotiation. To illustrate this, here is an extract from Forest and Pearpoint (1991) in Canada.

Exclusion: The unstated underlying assumptions of exclusion are, among others, that:

- We are not all equal in capacity or value.

- It is not feasible to give equal opportunity.

- We must choose and thus train an elite who will take care of 'the rest'.

- 'They' will benefit through the trickle-down theory.

Inclusion: People choosing inclusion look at whole systems and only label people by their names and their needs. Inclusion leaders foster cooperation and collaboration to solve problems while exclusion stresses competitiveness and individualism as the modus operandi. Inclusion works from opposite assumptions:

- We are unique in value; however, each has unique capacity.

- All people can learn.

- All people have contributions to make.

- We have a responsibility and an opportunity to give every person the chance to make a contribution.

It may be that a pupil with a physical disability is coming to your school and you find that the environment, both physical and social, requires considerable adjustment – this could be an uncomfortable situation, requiring changes of attitude as well as of procedure. Reviewing your school environment to include and provide suitable education for pupils with disabilities or illnesses will also improve the environment for everybody: it will make procedures more flexible and user friendly and it will make for a more humane and efficient working culture for staff and pupils alike (Forest and Pearpoint 1991, Rieser and Mason 1992, Rieser 1994, Cornwall 1995, Chapters 4–6).

Again, there are particular problems for the SENCO or other key members of staff in that pupils experiencing physical disabilities and medical conditions rarely proceed through these steps at a measured or measurable pace. On the one hand, a pupil may suffer the trauma of, say, a road traffic accident, which will disrupt their education considerably for a period of time. A period of rehabilitation and then reintegration may then be necessary in order to bring the pupil's educational life back to its previous routine. This does not fit in with graduated stages of assessment in the Code of Practice and may take a pupil to Stage 3 and beyond very quickly, requiring collaboration with outside agencies and so on. On the other hand, a pupil may have cerebral palsy with athetoid movements of the limbs. This is not an illness or a temporary condition. It is a condition that is permanent in a sense, but it can be alleviated and the functional difficulties considerably reduced by embedded and educational IEPs with adjustment to the school's physical and social environment.

In both the temporary conditions or illnesses and longer-term situations, planning is vital and relies upon good information being available to the planners. For example, the joint DfEE and Department of Health pack 'Supporting pupils with medical needs: a good practice guide' and Circular 14/96, 'Supporting pupils with medical needs in school', give guidance in:

- who is responsible for medication in schools;

- how to develop policies and procedures for supporting pupils with medical needs;

- dealing with medicines safely;

- drawing up a health care plan for a pupil with medical needs;

- common concerns such as asthma, diabetes and anaphylaxis;

- useful sets of proformas, contacts and help lines.

The legal framework

LEAs, schools and governing bodies are responsible for the health and safety of pupils in their care. The legal framework for schools dealing with the health and safety of *all* their pupils derives from health and safety legislation. *The law imposes duties on employers.* Other legislation, notably the 1993 Education Act and the 1968 Medicines Act, are also relevant to schools in dealing with pupils' medical needs. The following extracts outline the provisions of these Acts that are relevant to the health and safety of pupils.

- The 1974 Health and Safety at Work Act places duties on employers for the health and safety of their employees and anyone else on the premises. In schools this covers the head and teachers, non-teaching staff, pupils and visitors. Who the employer is depends on the type of school:

    the LEA is the employer in county and controlled schools;
    the governing body is the employer in city technology colleges and voluntary aided and grant maintained schools;
    the proprietor or the trustees are the employers in some independent schools.

    The main actions employers must take under the Health and Safety at Work Act are to:

    prepare a written health and safety management policy;
    make sure that staff are aware of the policy and their responsibilities within that policy;
    make sure that appropriate safety measures are in place;
    make sure that staff are properly trained and receive guidance on their responsibilities as employees.

- Most schools will at some time have pupils with medical needs on their roll. The responsibility of the employer is to make sure that *safety measures cover the needs of all pupils at the school.* This may mean making special arrangements for particular pupils.

- The 1992 Management of Health and Safety at Work Regulations require employers of staff at a school to:

make an assessment of the risks of activities;

introduce measures to control these risks;

tell their employees about these measures.

- In some cases pupils with medical needs may be more at risk than their classmates. The school may need to take additional steps to safeguard the health and safety of such pupils. In a few cases individual procedures may be needed. The employer is responsible for making sure that *all relevant staff know about and are, if necessary, trained to provide any additional support these pupils need.*

- *Pupils with medical needs will not necessarily have SEN.* Health authorities (HAs) should comply with a request for assistance from the LEA unless they decide not to do so on one of the grounds set out in Section 166 of the Education Act.

- *Help from the HA could include providing advice and training for school staff* in procedures to deal with a pupil's medical needs if that pupil would otherwise have limited access to education. Authorities and schools should work together, in close partnership with parents, to ensure proper support in school for pupils with medical needs.

- The 1968 Medicines Act places restrictions on dealings with medicinal products, including their administration. In the case of prescription-only medicines, anyone administering such a medicinal product by injection must be an appropriate practitioner (e.g. a doctor) or else must act in accordance with the practitioner's directions. There are exceptions for the administration of certain prescription-only medicines by injection in emergencies (in order to save life).

- Administering medicine or supervising a pupil taking it is a voluntary role. However, swift action would need to be taken by a member of staff to assist any pupil in an emergency.

- Teachers and other school staff in charge of pupils have a common law duty to act as any reasonably prudent parent would to make sure that pupils are healthy and safe on school premises and this might, in exceptional circumstances, extend to administering medicine and/or taking action in an emergency. This duty also extends to teachers leading activities taking place off the school site. Section 3(5) of the 1989 Children Act provides scope for teachers to do what is reasonable for the purpose of safeguarding or promoting children's welfare.

- The 1996 Education (School Premises) Regulations state that every school should have accommodation for medical or dental examination and treatment, and for the care of pupils during schools hours. It need not be used solely as medical accommodation, but it should be appropriate for that purpose and readily available for use as such when needed.

School policies and procedures for supporting pupils with medical needs

- *A clear policy understood and accepted by staff, parents and pupils and backed up by formal procedures* provides a sound basis for ensuring that pupils with medical needs receive proper care and support at school.

- The school's policy on supporting pupils who have medical needs or require medication in school should be *communicated to parents and to school staff.*

- *Parents are responsible for their child's medication.* The head is normally responsible for deciding whether the school can assist a pupil who needs medication. Such decisions should, as far as practicable, encourage regular attendance and full participation in school life.

- Children with *medical needs have the same rights of admission* to school as other children, and *cannot generally be excluded from school for medical reasons.*

- Many pupils with long-term medical conditions will be able to administer medicine themselves. *School policies should encourage this approach.*

- The local National Health Service (NHS) Trust can advise and support the school, pupils, parents, teachers and education welfare officers on health issues and advise them who the main health contact will be. The *main contact for schools is likely to be the school nurse.*

Drawing up an individual health care plan

- Some pupils have medical conditions that, if not properly managed, could limit their access to education. Such pupils are regarded as having *medical needs.* In some cases, schools will find it helpful to draw up individual procedures, in the form of a *health care plan in conjunction with the parents and health carers,* to ensure the safety of such pupils.

- They should set out in detail the measures needed to support a pupil in school, including preparing for an emergency situation.

- The information contained within the plans must be treated in confidence and should be used for no other purpose than for the school to set up a good support system.

Dealing with medicines safely

- Particular attention must be paid to the safe storage, handling and disposal of medicines. Training for staff should include guidance in safety procedures. Some medication must be readily available in an emergency and should not be locked away. Relevant school staff and the pupil concerned should know where the medication is kept.

A pupil with a physical disability such as cerebral palsy may not need medical supervision. It is not an illness and the education of such a pupil may not require any medical oversight at all. The balance between the pupil's educational, social and health needs is very important for his/her development. There is a difference between health professionals (physiotherapy, occupational and speech therapy and nursing) and doctors (GPs, consultants, etc.) giving medical advice. They have different roles and functions; it is important not to confuse them. On the other hand, a pupil may have an allergy where the medical advice is vital, sometimes for the sake of life and limb. The relative balance of, and need for, medical advice should be considered carefully, in partnership with the pupil's parents. For example, anaphylactic reactions (a severe reaction to one or a number of causes such as wasp or bee stings, nut allergies, ingestion, inhalation or injection or skin contact with particular substances) can be extreme. There are many different causes and if the reaction is seen in dramatic form it may sometimes be confused with 'panic attacks', where difficulties in breathing cause the panic. In these cases, it is pro-active planning and preparedness that are important as well as monitoring and the pupil themselves being a major part of the solution in learning about their own illness.

SENCOs will need to check that *pro-active systems and procedures are in place* and that one new pupil or new situation will not require a complete overhaul of the school's responses. Sudden as incidences of illness or accidents may be, the school should be able to respond through established strategies and procedures:

A clear policy understood and accepted by staff, parents and pupils provides a sound basis for ensuring that children with medical needs receive proper care and support at school. Policies should, as far as possible, enable regular school attendance. Formal systems and procedures drawn up in partnership with parents and staff should back up the policy.

(DfEE and Department of Health 1996)

The school is asked in the Code of Practice (1994) to state clearly when assessment is needed and to make arrangements in an orderly fashion for individual pupils to be assessed. This poses two completely different types of problems for the school and the SENCO. When a sudden event or illness overtakes a pupil, the needs of the moment often put great pressure on all concerned. It is vitally important in this situation that a school has a robust and consensual approach with effective policies and guidelines, combined with good relationships and a well thought out ethos concerning flexibility in organisation and procedures, relationships, behaviour, attitudes and personal development of its pupils. On the other hand, a school may have to face difficult questions about the long-term physical, emotional and academic development of a pupil who is physically disabled and who will be in the school for a number of years. The need for quick assessment and response is less important than a considered longer-term approach that provides equality of opportunity and access to the curriculum as a whole. It may be that once strategies have been put in place, through the IEP development, they will continue from year to year. There is a need to monitor the school's responses at all times and to make adjustments or consider more training or staff development.

In order not to be continually reactive, the school management or the SENCO or key worker should attempt to establish useful links with outside agencies as an *on-going process and in advance of the necessity to work together, if possible*. In most cases of physical disability and illness (whether developmental coordination difficulty or a degenerative illness like muscular dystrophy) it will be necessary to seek outside advice and this may set in motion a process of referral. Mainstream schools need a framework which incorporates a clear policy, early identification of physical disabilities and medical conditions, interventions with stated aims and a simple and clear set of procedures that are known to all. Early identification of a disability that is not obvious, such as developmental coordination difficulties (also called minimal motor impairment), may well avoid many problems and emotional pain for the pupil at a later date. It requires a sharp and knowledgeable eye on academic and social development.

It may take some time to get policies into place and longer to use training and staff meetings to help colleagues become familiar with them and to be able to put them into action. At the end of the day, the benefits will be felt among all pupils, their parents and the staff of the school. In a culture of acceptance and belonging for pupils whose needs are different from the majority, they are only regarded as 'exceptional' or 'special' or, worse still, a nuisance and a problem, by those who adhere to an unfashionable and somewhat outdated view of schools and education. The majority of children will have additional needs of one sort or another, and to varying degrees, at some point in their school careers.

Referral, and the first question is: Whom do you refer to?

It may be that a pupil with a disability or medical condition is admitted to the school or becomes ill and is under the initial scrutiny of medical services or already has a diagnosis to which the school will respond. The teacher learns of this from other sources and then makes suitable adjustments. On the other hand the teacher may, through knowing the pupil and through daily observation, become concerned about some aspect of the pupil's physical, emotional or academic development or about progress on the work given. The first step will be to discuss this within the school between relevant members of staff and with the SENCO. The next stage is referral to groups, agencies and professionals outside the school. These may be some, or all, of the following.

• *School psychological service and independent specialist psychological advice* when appropriate	• Local or regional *hospital school service* (or service for sick children) for on-going support and advice about illness
• On-going *partnership with parents*	• Any *peripatetic support teams* in the area
• National and local *voluntary groups* with specialist knowledge	• *Education welfare service*
• The *school health service* (e.g. for advice about medication, etc.)	• *Therapy services* (speech and language therapy, physiotherapy and occupational therapy)
• The *child mental health service*	• *Social services* (e.g. child protection and custody issues)
• Links with *other schools and/or colleges*	• *SEN learning support services*

Consultation and observation

Consultation is a time for the support services, consultant or outside agency to listen, where schools and their staff express their concerns. It may be necessary for outside personnel to meet the appropriate school staff, collect information, make some observations and arrange a meeting within a set time to plan for the future. The school staff and SENCO should think about the pupil's broad physical, social and emotional needs as well as possible short-term targets. Parents, health professionals, social workers and any other appropriate agencies should be invited to joint planning meetings. Issues around pupils' academic and physical needs, attendance and pupils' views will also be discussed here.

Joint planning

The joint planning meeting should underpin all subsequent work. How it goes will depend on whether the school assessment is at Stage 2 or 3 or whether the pupil already has a statement. These meetings should be well prepared, and this depends a great deal on the effectiveness of the existing IEP planning and evaluation. If it is good, people will know what to expect and the meeting will be more effective. Time boundaries are as important as clear outcomes. The pupil's broad academic, physical, social and emotional needs can be outlined and realistic, short-term, meaningful targets identified. The real work, however, is done in negotiating the process – the 'who does what, where, when and how' – and it is important to reflect this in the IEP somewhere so that proper evaluation of the response to the situation is recorded. Often the recording does not monitor the *effectiveness of any outside interventions*, only that they have happened.

It is essential that parents and others are included in the planning e.g. learning support assistant, parent, education welfare officer, (residential) social worker, educational psychologist, hospital school teacher and SENCO and that all relevant parties, including the class teacher, *remain* responsible for their part in the process. This will be determined by:

- the pupil's educational needs;
- the teacher's needs to make the curriculum available;

- the educational target(s) and outcomes decided upon;
- available resources.

The teacher will alter the teaching and differentiate the work and the organisational aspects of the classroom, as appropriate. Immediate support could be in-class, whole-class, small group, personal management needs, individual work, staff supervision, INSET or therapy and health support sessions. Support from other agencies might involve physiotherapy or occupational therapy, speech therapy, counselling, child guidance or medical and specialist medical advice, to name but a few. It is vital to evaluate the effectiveness of the support in reaching the agreed targets and in supporting the child's educational development. Once the process is agreed and everyone is aware of their role, it is formally recorded and logged on the IEP. This process is integrally linked to the writing of IEPs and to daily planning. The major success of joint planning is that it gives staff time to think and *provides an opportunity to develop a response to the necessary social and environmental adjustments rather than a reaction to them.*

Monitoring and review

The joint planning meetings should always set a review date which is also logged and evaluated on the IEP. Particularly for a school, pupil or parent new to the process, regular reviews are important (for example, to be set within 2 weeks of the joint plan). This helps to support and encourage. It irons out any minor difficulties and keeps communication open. The termly or half-termly review process is much easier to conduct and assess as it is directly related to the targets set. The process itself should also be reviewed. It becomes clear who has done what, how, where and when and what the results are. The teacher's daily planning and assessment of progress are crucial to the refining of IEP targets at all stages in this process. Given that a statement has 'annual targets' the whole cycle should fit together as one continuous process.

Classroom assistants and learning support

Classroom assistants do have an important role to play in helping children to learn. However, exactly what this role should be, given the levels of training currently provided, is not always clear. The apparent belief by Government that anyone can teach young children is misguided and reflects a lack of understanding of what the role of teacher and the concept of teaching embrace. Teachers are in control of all aspects of the planning cycle of children's learning, but classroom assistants are expected to intervene and to direct and (informally) assess learning without prior knowledge of planning or organisation in other elements of the cycle. For classroom assistants to be more effective in supporting both teachers and children, they need to be much more involved in the planning cycle. Equally, the teachers need to intervene and assess more, so that they have a clear picture of all the elements upon which to base their planning. A further inescapable outcome is that the classroom assistant has neither sufficient time nor knowledge to formulate and articulate the outcomes of children's experiences other than in 'product' terms.

Classroom assistants' support of statemented children raises other questions such as the dependency of the child on adult support. Labelling of children is also found to be a problem if classroom assistants are perceived to exist solely for those children. Consideration needs to be given to the quality and equity of children's experiences if they are being taught for a major part of the time by a classroom assistant who does not have the teacher's training in developing suitable activities to meet the child's developmental and curriculum needs. It is vital that schools (and Government) help classroom assistants to evolve a unique identity, the components of which should include generalist elements applicable to all, but specific aspects for those who are capable of more. There is a need for a proper career structure which takes into account individual strengths and personal circumstances.

Organisational change

Implementing organisational change, even with clear goals and plans of action, is a complex process. In order to grow and develop, particularly in terms of expecting staff to develop their abilities and commitment to recording progress for individual pupils through IEPs, there will need to be some organisational or group (attitudes, skills and understanding) changes. Sometimes the SENCO or other responsible person will find it necessary to motivate change in order to set up a satisfactory system for coordinating and monitoring IEPs. To *energise changes*, it might be necessary to do some or all of the following.

- *Identify surface dissatisfaction with the present system.* Changes are usually (but not always) energised by problems or difficulties. This is a difficult area for SENCOs, senior responsible teachers and, eventually, senior management. It requires careful planning, often with supportive external advice, in order to present the positive side of changes and subsequent benefits all round.

- *Ensure overall participation in change.* Problem solving and solution generating strategies must involve as many staff, parents and other relevant professionals as possible – as part of the solutions. Participation will ensure that changes are integral to people's work, fully understood and adopted as far as possible in any given circumstances. They will be more realistic and realisable.

- *Reward behaviour in support of change.* Sometimes the benefits of a new system, procedure or attitude are not always immediately apparent. In this case, it may be necessary for the SENCO to focus in-school support on activities and staff who are moving towards the school's policy or more coherent strategies for pupils. Often when the benefits of new systems or strategies begin to take effect, this will become more self-perpetuating. If it does not then review and adjustments may be necessary.

- *Time and opportunity are needed to prepare and disengage from present way(s) of doing things or seeing things.* People get stuck in their ways and they often need time to consider what is happening. They need this time in order not to feel deskilled or marginalised – with proper handling and consideration, new skills and approaches can be fostered.

Teamwork

The relationship between the functioning of an effective team and its effect on both pupils and adults in schools and units is a mutual one. Positive social behaviour, to gain access to learning for young people, is influenced by the 'models' provided by adults, which in turn dictate the 'school culture' and ethos. The culture of a school and the ethos under which staff work will affect the use, efficiency and manageability of the IEP process. In pp. 1–19 there was a clear focus on equality of opportunity and an understanding of the way in which social attitudes and often personal prejudice will impact upon the opportunities available to individual pupils through IEPs and skilled teaching. However, our focus is on IEPs and, when teamwork is good, group life is enriched by positive and enthusiastic interchange on a regular basis and there are many opportunities to share and develop the valuable information that IEPs can give. It is also more efficient to share and develop consistent practices across a school – it radically reduces the individual effort in the long run. There will inevitably be many barriers to communication on both an interpersonal and a whole-school front that will make IEPs more time-consuming and their monitoring more difficult. To develop good teamwork it is often beneficial to bring in outside training or consultants to work with the staff team, as a whole.

Coordination and monitoring: Institutional self-review

The National Curriculum is a basic framework for academic and subject-based education. The development of a whole person goes much further than this and is recognised in the OFSTED framework for the inspection of schools (1996). There are other important aspects such as the pupil's or student's 'spiritual, cultural and moral development'. The school should have an active equal opportunities policy and there are other aspects of the school that impact upon the lives of pupils and students with disabilities. These should be checked (see Table 16).

Some basic conditions to check – whole-school aspects	Results of your review. Are these areas understood? Is effective action taken?
The *behaviour and attitudes of others* in the school and the general ethos of the school in promoting equality of opportunity and inclusive practices.	
Community links so that the pupils do not become isolated in a specific (perhaps over-protective, perhaps too harsh) environment. Contacts with the world outside school are important.	
Transitional arrangements: 'accepting' a pupil occurs at the outset and 'belonging' depends on well handled arrangements and decisions.	
Personal care, health education and social skills mean staff understanding *the nature of 'independence'* and 'enablement'. Pupils having some degree of control.	
Motor development, physical therapy or movement activity – a balance between the various aspects of a pupil's development is achieved (e.g. academic, social, health and physical).	
All children need support in their *emotional development through good relationships* with their peers and with adults . . . how are these pupils supported?	
Personal autonomy through choice and opportunity is vital to sustain motivation and good social development.	
Additional learning support (e.g. medical and therapy) services being consistent and integrated.	
Gaps in perceptual–motor development and school experience are understood and catered for in planning IEPs and targets.	

Table 16

Two examples of IEPs – (1) and (2)

Look at the two examples on these pages and consider . . .
How do the designs of these IEPs reflect the following, for example?

1. Recording parent's or pupil's views and contribution?
2. Evaluating the response of outside professionals and its effectiveness?
3. Enabling the school to match the support given to academic success and progress?
4. Useful information to monitor the differentiation of lesson or learning activities?
5. Information to monitor the medium-term progress of pupils?
6. Information to refine longer-term educational targets?
7. Triggers and/or steps in the referral process?
8. The extent of outside agency involvement?
9. The quality and focus of outside professionals' interventions?

Be critical of the layout and content. What do you think of their usefulness?

CODE OF PRACTICE: INDIVIDUAL EDUCATION PLAN (1)

Individual education plan for:	DOB:	NC year:	Level statement

Term 19	Key members of staff

Nature of the child's learning difficulty:

Provision made:	Staff involved:

Involvement of other agencies/external specialists including frequency and timing of support:

Specific curricular programmes (including NC requirements) and learning activities and strategies to be used:

Materials:	Equipment:

Targets to be achieved:

By:

Help from parents at home:	Pastoral care or medical requirements:

Monitoring and assessment arrangements:	Review Date:
	Signed..Head teacher
	....Special educational needs coordinator

Date:

INDIVIDUAL EDUCATION PLAN (2)

Name		Date of birth		NC yr		Audit		
Key worker			Form tutor					
Those present at review meeting		PRIORITIES: In addition to a broadly balanced curriculum key areas of need are:						
Targets	Action plan			Lead professional		Termly review (date)		

TARGET SHEET	Name:
Concept(s)	Lead professional
Overall aim	IEP TARGET
Baseline	
Steps to target (by number)	Instructions
Materials/strategies/facilities	Criteria for success
	Practice/over learning

Recording	Start date	Review date

Date	Notes	Date	Notes

Coordination and monitoring: Ideas for action

Monitoring by SENCO and colleagues of the effect of the IEP and the effect on the IEP for pupils with physical disabilities and medical conditions.

SENCO and/or 'key' personnel for pastoral care, physical disabilities and medical conditions	Classroom or learning support assistants	Head and senior management (including governors)	Outside agencies and professions	Teaching colleagues
The day-to-day operation of the school's SEN, pastoral and equal opportunity policies	The general arrangements in school for playtimes or break times and pupils' opportunities to participate fully in the social life of the school.	Focus on efficient use of IEP in meetings, conferences or in collaboration between staff in achieving policy aims and intentions.	The arrangements for outside interventions and the way these are recorded and integrated into the IEP. Evaluation of the quality of outcomes for pupils.	The impact of class teaching on pupils' progress and attainment in specific subjects or activities. Pupils' responses to teaching and recording these.
Liaising with and advising fellow teachers	About deployment of classroom assistants/learning support assistants and requirements for daily information to be collated for IEPs.	Sensitive arrangements for consistent recording of difficult incidents or general progress towards IEP targets.	Working out special arrangements (e.g. timetable) with teachers for outside interventions or professional visits.	Access strategies, differentiation of lessons and activities – pupil responses recorded on IEP and evaluated.
Coordinating provision for children experiencing physical disabilities and medical conditions	**What is the classroom assistant's/learning support assistant's role?** In classroom? In the school during playtimes/lunch? Support staff and parents have a responsibility for monitoring the pupil's physical well-being.	Sufficient allocation and efficient management of resources to support IEP targets for physical disabilities and medical conditions.	Ensuring confidentiality and good professional collaboration. Protecting educational priorities on IEP (e.g. monitoring the disruption to pupil's education).	The implementation of IEP targets in lessons through effective teaching practices. Efficient day-to-day assessment towards IEP targets.
Maintaining the school's SEN register and overseeing the records on all pupils with physical disabilities and medical conditions	The 'flow' of information from the IEP(s) to individual classroom assistants/ learning support assistants to support focused and additional teaching activity.	Good information coming from IEPs supports legal requirements for annual review. Matching IEP targets with efficient use of resources.	Regular reviews of concerns or progress stemming from outside interventions. The impact of other interventions on progress towards IEP targets.	The arrangements for teachers to show concerns stemming from IEP-related activities. The flow of information about IEPs and special arrangements.

Liaising with the parents of children with physical disabilities and medical conditions	Direct lines of communication with parents – nature of guidance. Daily links with parents through home books, etc. – **links with** IEP arrangements and targets.	The flow of information from the school in general to parents. Involvement of senior management team with appropriate and pre-arranged activities or interventions to support IEP targets.	IEP targets and information and match with **information to parents** about specialist groups or support.	Accuracy and sensitivity of reporting to parents and progress towards IEP targets. Relaying of parental concerns quickly and sensitively. Positive responses to parental concerns.
Contributing to in-service training of all staff in matters relating to physical disabilities and medical conditions	Consult and assess training needs in relation to IEP targets and common elements. **Contribute their perspective as advocate for the pupil in all training situations.**	The sufficiency and targeting of resources for training on IEP-related areas. Advise senior management team/ governing body on this. Arrangements for INSET and its impact on whole-school developments.	The group or common IEP elements or targets – match **outside trainers or consultants** to staff needs in these areas. Match providers and external agencies with specialist knowledge.	Consult and assess training needs in relation to IEP targets and common elements. Arrangements for INSET and the outcomes of INSET – its impact in the classroom.

Monitoring the impact of school management on IEPs

Monitor IEP support . . .	**Monitor activities and review effectiveness . . .** **(1) Well established** **(2) Need development**	**Comment and take action(s) . . . *(e.g. your comment)***
Overall school management	● Establishing and maintaining internal and external communication systems *e.g. (2)* ● Staff management – sometimes complicated procedures ● Fostering a sense of community with genuine acceptance and belonging for all ● Taking the lead in setting aims and standards ● Supporting staff in understanding diverse pupil needs ● Directing overall curriculum and organisational planning ● Establish rules and procedures but enable flexibility for change ● Encouraging 'community' through collective responsibility for all children ● Develop and outline the personal and social curriculum ● Provide models of inclusive attitudes and behaviour – e.g. each of us is unique with skills and capabilities ● Procedures and teaching practices consistent with the RE and PSHE policies of the school	*Establish regular (weekly or monthly) meetings with therapy team . . .*

Monitor IEP support . . .	Monitor activities and review effectiveness . . . (1) Well established (2) Need development	Comment and take action(s) . . . (e.g. your comment)
Successful policies for inclusion	• Based on a clear and defensible set of principles or values encouraging equality of opportunity and inclusion • Encourage effective partnerships and a culture of partnership rather than 'help' • Deal with attitudes, behaviour and procedures specific to that school • Strike a healthy balance between the medical and social or educational needs of the pupil • Reserve the most severe punishments, e.g. exclusion, for the most serious offences, e.g. violence • Allow for flexibility in the administration of punishments to take account of individual needs	
Enabling IEP targets . . .	• Assist pupils in making decisions for themselves • Avoid practices that encourage passivity, pity or over-protection • Will focus or include adjustments to the physical and social environment as well as individual factors • Recognise the importance of the role of parents and of all support staff • Increase access and apply to school activities on and off site	
Particular incidents affecting IEP targets . . .	• Be alert to signs of social exclusion – bullying and teasing or harassment • The level of debate needs to be raised from details of organisation into genuinely inclusive strategies • Lack of knowledge and natural discussion about disability and illness	
Pastoral care and personal development	• Senior pastoral staff should spend more time advising and supporting colleagues, and they need to have a clear and cultural view of inclusive practice • Tutor periods should be used well, rather than just being seen as a time-killing exercise • The pastoral system should also be used to provide feedback on pupils' views • Good communication links should be developed between pastoral staff and support services. • Continuing professional development should develop teachers' basic counselling and interpersonal skills • Senior pastoral staff should have more in-depth training or qualifications in this area	

Coordinating the physical and social environment

At one time physical access was thought to be the main, if not the only, requirement for pupils to be included in a mainstream school. It is now realised that physical access alone is not enough. Even when this basic requirement was acknowledged, many secondary schools were built on two or three floors, without lifts or adaptations, making access impossible to a large proportion of classrooms. Primary schools are much more commonly on one level. Each school will have its own unique set of circumstances in terms of buildings and facilities. The list of points to check in Table 17 are not exhaustive but point to the broader consequences of lack of physical access and contain some suggestions for improving access.

Action needed . . .	Working with attitudes	Procedures, resources and actions
The classroom may need to be reorganised . . .	Physical changes or 'rules' should be introduced through discussion and with the cooperation of other members of the class. They need to understand the need behind the request.	. . . to accommodate specialised equipment such as laptops, communicators, frames, wheelchairs or special desktop adaptations.
Physical adaptations should be decided . . .	Discussion with pupils themselves as well as specialist architectural or building expertise. Careful handling needed to make sure child is listened to and needs of school fulfilled by experts.	Is it, for instance, necessary to install or arrange: (a) special toileting facilities; (b) ramps; (c) grab rails; (d) a lift (or modification in classroom usage)?
The pupil must be as independent as possible . . .	It is important that the *teaching space* allows the pupil to move around as independently as possible and become an accepted social member of the group.	Any equipment needed by pupils should be as unobtrusive as possible and not constitute a physical barrier to spontaneous interaction.
Suitable seating must be available . . .	*Pupils can outgrow furniture* and the arrangements need to be regularly monitored. Also, there may be differing needs in different (subject) areas of the school.	Pupils must have stable, secure seating at the right height and may also need tables adjusted so that wheelchairs can get under them.
● **Are there quiet areas in the class . . .** ● **. . . and areas for social interchange in the school?**	● This is particularly important for pupils or students with additional perceptual problems where individual pupils can improve their concentration on the task in hand. ● Are these completely accessible? Are any pupils denied access to play and recreational spaces in or outside the building?	
Is there a suitable place for eating meals (not segregated away or alone)?	This will require cooperation from other members of staff (e.g. dinner ladies) and will require discussion with pupil (and peers) about how to handle this situation.	Consideration for a person who may have some problems with eating and drinking. A pupil or student may need to manage their mealtimes without hustle and bustle but without missing out on the social aspects of mealtimes.

Are toilets satisfactory . . . and bathing or showering facilities?	Are pupil's dignity and privacy properly respected – even though they may require assistance at times? Do the facilities also encourage respect for pupil's dignity and privacy?	Are all the facilities within reach and usable, easily accessible? Are they large enough and private? Are there rails for independent transfers? Are all things required (e.g. chain/handle, taps, paper, soap) within reach? Is there an alarm system to call for help if required?
Consideration, time and effort . . . timetabling and joint planning	Time is a finite resource. Pupils need to be able to work with teachers and support staff to make sure their time is also used productively. This requires both sensitive consideration of the pupil's individual needs and larger considerations of school timetabling. Priorities identified and time used well. A balance between individual circumstances and opportunities to participate in the school curriculum.	*Extra time* may be required for a variety of purposes, for example to overcome specific problems (i.e. stairs, doors, seats), for specific tasks like communicating and recording work or moving between lessons, for personal hygiene or dressing and undressing, for visiting professionals, etc. Never underestimate the small and seemingly insignificant problems that can become large ones.
Freedom of movement, whether assisted or independent, is of the greatest importance . . .	Moving and lifting others who cannot do this for themselves should not be an unwanted back-breaking chore that makes everyone feel incapable. It should become a joint exercise involving efficiency of movement, planning in stages and comfort or security for the person who is being moved.	Make the connection between developing your own efficient and useful movement and helping others to move and balance. Being aware of the inefficiency and instability of our own movements can only help in terms of approaching the difficulties of others with some humility and understanding.
When planning timetables at secondary level . . .	Sometimes compromises will have to be made but the main priority should always be maximum inclusion in curricular and social activities. Consideration will have to be given to the location and accessibility of rooms for pupils in wheelchairs or with difficulties in getting about.	Consideration given to: ● rooms on split sites or different levels; ● the pupil or student leaving the lesson before the end; ● homework not being given at the end (or pupil having alternative arrangements); ● lessons moved to an accessible area (when specialist equipment is not needed).

Table 17 (continued overleaf)

The pupil's individual timetable needs to be coordinated . . .	This should be discussed with a 'key' person, class teacher or coordinator. The school's senior management team should be able to support adjustments to a pupil's timetables for specific reasons. Does the timetable achieve agreed educational objectives and targets for that pupil?	To achieve the proper balance of curriculum subjects, group activities, individual input, specialist learning, therapy programmes, meetings and extra-curricular work. *The pupil's individual pace* of learning and factors such as fatigue need to be reflected in the timetable.
Wheelchair maintenance and use . . .	Does the pupil plan with adults what she/he needs to carry around? Does the pupil (begin to) take some responsibility for checking the condition of the chair and its accessories? How does the pupil feel about the chair and its use? Do they have any new ideas about this?	Are all the parts on the wheelchair? Are the tyres properly inflated? Is it clean? Do the brakes work? Is the seat in good condition and clean? Can the pupil or student carry things (e.g. books, equipment, communicator) on the wheelchair?

Table 17 (cont.)

Involving the learner: Principles

Involving children in their IEPs is also a good way of embedding IEPs into the system. If children expect to be involved in their IEP, staff will continue to use them.

(Tod *et al.* 1998)

In order to derive meaningful IEP targets, the primary concern is, by involving the learner, to gain some understanding of the internal and environmental factors and circumstances impacting on the learner and to do three things with this knowledge:

- to understand and be able to use appropriate language and descriptors of the learner's needs to generate both targets *and evaluative statements* for IEPs;

- to match the learner's needs with reasonable adjustments to the environment (physical, social and organisational) and appropriate planned action by the teacher and the school, through the IEPs;

- to make certain that the learner's progress is charted and shared in a meaningful way in the context of longer-term curriculum goals, and to raise their standard of academic success.

UN Convention on the Rights of the Child (1989): *Article 12* states the right of the child to express an opinion and to have that opinion taken into account, in any matter or procedure affecting the child.

Involving the learner means making the process of learning accessible and meaningful to them and helping the learner to gain an understanding, and motivation, from knowing where they are trying to get to, *in the longer term.* Pupils will work if they feel there are going to be visible benefits and some will work for benefits that will be seen in the future. Involving the learner also means that the learner begins to take responsibility for themselves and their own learning. This is important for all children but is crucially important for pupils with physical disabilities and medical conditions. Why? Because they need to become independent learners. The word independence, as explored earlier, does not mean doing everything for yourself – none of us does that. We all use aids, adaptations, tools and other people to help us achieve our goals in life. To take responsibility for yourself is first of all to begin to solve your own problems and secondly to use what resources (personal and material) you have available to do this. This is a skilled and energetic approach to life – not one that relies on having things done for you, or believes in allowing others to restrict your opportunities by labelling or discriminating against you because of your physical or medical characteristics. This is all very well in ethical and philosophical terms but what does it mean in practice? The process is considerably enhanced when the learner is able to contribute a view, for example on the priorities for target setting or the balance of individual versus subject targets but involvement becomes vital in ensuring access and participation. In order to be involved and contribute effectively, to take responsibility for his or her own learning and growing independence, *the learner has to feel competent.*

Becoming competent

This is a complex process, involving many factors within the learner and many in the situation that the learner finds himself or herself. A lot of the time we have to work intuitively but, as any athlete will tell you, in order to improve our competence, skills and understanding, it is necessary to become aware of areas for further development in ourselves. For example, working alongside a person who has great difficulties communicating or who uses technology to communicate can make both parties feel incompetent unless there is confidence in the process itself – even when the technology does not work well. Poor experiences in communication can have a very significant effect on a person's self-image and self-esteem. It is also vital that *adults recognise and make clear their own existing skills and abilities and then discover areas for growth and development*. We can then develop confidence from this knowledge and *celebrate our own competence*. It is also very important that the notion of 'independent learning' is adjusted and understood in this context. For example, a pupil may have to remain at home for a substantial period after hospitalisation because of sudden illness. He or she is then thrown into a situation where it is necessary to take responsibility for his or her own learning because the continuous support of a school routine is no longer there. It cannot be achieved alone. Home support might involve placing a fax machine at home so that work can be marked and annotated in between home visits. Adult and pupil must work together to achieve progress and access not only to academic or subject-based learning, but also to the development of socially skilful independence and to personal development generally.

It is important, at this stage, to be aware that 'physical management' and 'setting targets' comprise more than just observing, analysing and including therapy strategies into the IEP process. *Teachers' and other adults' actions, beliefs and attitudes* also play an important part in the whole process. Decisions have to be made and careful discrimination is necessary to separate 'teacher targets' (in managing the consequences of the individual's condition or disability) from 'learner targets' (in developing new knowledge, understanding, skills, beliefs and behaviour, for example). To get these muddled could lead to an adult equating their need to 'manage' the situation with an appropriate target for the pupil – they are not the same. For example, a teacher may 'encourage the use of alternative communication systems' whereas the pupil is 'learning to initiate communication by contributing spontaneously to the weekend news session' on the path to becoming a more independent learner.

Self-esteem and the 'messages' we convey

A full consideration of this aspect of the learner is not appropriate in this book and can be found in Cornwall (1995, 1996) and in Cornwall and Tod (1998). However, the impact of a disability or the consequences of a medical condition or illness can have a significant effect on lowering the pupil's self-esteem and can be a suitable area for IEP targets. Teachers, enablers or assistants, parents and carers need to be aware of the ideas and feelings that a pupil is developing towards themselves, their capabilities and their worth as a person. A pupil with low self-esteem finds it difficult to try new strategies. He protects what he has and continues to behave in a manner consistent with his poor views of himself. If a pupil feels rejected and views *himself as unacceptable* and valueless then he does not necessarily regard disapproval as a reaction to his disability or condition, *but to himself*. Pupils with low self-esteem will look for information to confirm a poor view of themselves.

Reactions that may be indicative of low self-esteem:

- Wishes he/she were someone else.
- Finds it difficult to make decisions.
- Appears anxious.
- Socially isolated.
- Lacks confidence.
- Rarely laughs or smiles.
- Gets upset by personal mistakes.
- Rigid in thinking.
- Finds it difficult to work independently.

The importance of a good understanding of self-esteem for teachers lies in the formulating of targets. Targets for IEPs need to be couched in measurable terms and strategies can then emanate from them. A suitable target for the learner could be: 'able to distinguish between areas where he can succeed and those that he finds difficult'. Some pupils and young people have come to believe that achievement and success are not only impossible but completely out of their control. What is more, there is probably a deep-seated belief that they have no influence or impact on what goes on around them or on events in their life. Self-esteem is not a panacea to changing the pupil. It has less to do with any internal impairment of emotion or personality than with the impact of other people, significant, and less significant and including social exclusion, conditioning and cultural factors. If none of the external factors changes then internal constructs will not change either.

On becoming 'an independent learner'

Independence is defined too frequently by the ability to carry out certain physical tasks without help. This definition of independence is fundamentally flawed. First, it focuses on physical capacities to the exclusion of psychological and social dimensions of independence. We might ask what the point is of having the physical ability without the psychological wherewithal or the opportunity to put skills into practice. Secondly, the underlying philosophy of this approach is that disabled people have an impairment whose effects need to be minimised or 'fixed' towards an able-bodied 'norm'. This is what Fenton and Hughes (1989) call the 'fix-it' approach. This provides the yardstick by which disabled people are judged and found second best: a process which helps perpetuate psychological and social dependence. In order to generate meaningful targets and strategies for an IEP it is necessary to develop an alternative definition of independence which is sufficiently flexible to enable disabled pupils to explore what independence means for them. *This definition starts from the premise that the key to independence is choice.* The issue is having control over how, when and in what circumstances help is given. It also allows the fact that disabled pupils are capable of choice and self-direction. It is a social issue not an individual problem. *It explicitly recognises that empowerment is an issue for all – disabled people, parents and carers, helpers, professionals, friends and so on.* Moreover, the model is holistic (i.e. not definable by any one of its constituent parts). All attributes are given equal weight. Similarly, one of the messages communicated is that *disabled pupils and those with medical conditions cannot be defined by their perceived physical attributes alone and should be perceived as whole people* (Fenton and Hughes 1989).

It is crucial that teachers, professionals and support staff feel empowered enough to surrender the decision making and power they exercise on behalf of pupils with physical disabilities and medical conditions. *It is important that all staff are encouraged to examine their own assumptions, beliefs and susceptibility to broader social and political pressures.* They are not immune from holding devaluing attitudes which translate into actions and comments that reduce empowerment, choice and opportunity. The development of an *empowering school ethos is a prerequisite* to enabling disabled pupils to achieve independence. This, more than anything, involves the participation and involvement of pupils in assessment procedures right through to the setting of targets and problem solving activities. Pupils need to develop the ability to become *'controllers of their help'* (Fenton and Hughes 1989).

- Teachers will need to strike a balance between traditional academic targets and personal and social education.

- In a well integrated mainstream school, with good pastoral and other support systems, the personal and emotional needs of pupils with disabilities or medical conditions will not be overlooked. The differences of disability or medical needs will not be denied in an ill thought out rush to provide absolute equality of treatment, rather than equality of opportunity.

- The implementation of an empowering approach through IEPs will involve teachers, support staff, parents and the pupils themselves in planning, assessment and review procedures where no one is working in isolation or in ignorance of the roles of others.

- The process of monitoring and developing IEPs, the annual review process and that of planning for differentiation in lessons give opportunities to involve the learner and to discuss issues arising from active participation in the curriculum and the general life of the school.

Students as controllers of their help

The transition from living a life as others want (dependence) to living it as the adolescent wants to live (independence) is extraordinarily difficult for most teenagers and their families. The difficulty is compounded in the case of adolescents with disabilities.

[The] key to independence . . . is CHOICE: choosing to complete physical tasks without assistance or choosing to complete physical tasks with assistance whilst being in control of how and when that assistance is offered.

(Adapted from Fenton and Hughes 1989)

It is important that helpers of *younger students* with disabilities encourage them to make decisions about whether they want help or not, and which part of the task they want help with and which part they can manage on their own. Equally, for younger students it may be important to encourage them to try things themselves as much as possible. *Older students* should be encouraged to choose if they need help or not with a particular task, on a particular day – depending on how they feel. They need to be able then to negotiate with the helper, efficiently and politely. When working with a student with a disability on any task, it is necessary to explore together the possible ways of helping. The student can then choose for this task, with this helper, on this day, in this context, at this time, how much help she/he wants.

Involving assisted communicators . . .

(With acknowledgements to and extracts from Thomas 1995.)

Participation in the classroom requires communication, and if communication goes awry it will affect intellectual growth, social interaction, language development and emotional attitude. A significant number of young people are unable to speak or write because of a physical disability, language disorder or learning difficulty and, without significant adjustments, these will affect the involvement of the learner in the classroom and school life. In a 1989 Office for Population Census and Surveys (OPCS) survey there were an estimated 121,000 children with communication disabilities in Great Britain. Communication that occurs in educational contexts happens in oral, verbal and non-verbal modes; it is not just what is spoken but also the way we communicate, sending out unspoken messages about what we think (usually of each other). For pupils who require assistance, our role is to facilitate the communication, and therefore the involvement in the education, that occurs in the classroom. Within a class there may be several pupils or perhaps only one pupil using augmentative or alternative communication systems such as picture and symbol charts, word and spelling boards, gesture and signing systems, eye pointing or electronic voice output aids. *Most of these pupils will use a combination of assistive techniques*, rather than one exclusively, and many will use some vocalisation or speech. In order to enable involvement and participation, there are four main stages to go through.

1. *Identify communication needs and communication skills.* The identification of current patterns of participation within the classroom is a practical and systematic approach which can provide the opportunity to reassess both the pupil and the educational environment. It may be a yearly exercise involving the multi-disciplinary team which supports the young person as well as the user themselves.

2. *Assess opportunity and access barriers.* When the optimal level of participation has been agreed, it is necessary to examine the possible barriers to that participation. This will include an examination of not only the pupil's performance, but also the policies, practices, attitudes, knowledge, skills and resources of the educational environment.

3. *Plan and implement intervention.* This is the action plan. It should clearly identify what programmes need to be implemented, who is responsible for each programme and the time-scale for implementation.

4. *Evaluate intervention.* As with the implementation of any programme, judging effectiveness for both the pupil and the support team is critical. At this point it may be necessary to reassess elements of the programme or plan new interventions, so completing a cycle of the process.

Activation and motivation

The following is a list of attributes, taken from sport psychology (Bakker *et al.* 1990) and in different forms used by athletes to improve their performance. The lessons learned in top competition are as relevant to pupils with physical disabilities or conditions as to anyone and point the way to *involving the learner actively in his or her own growth and development*. When learning or engaging in classroom and other educational activities, as far as possible, the pupil should:

- share or make the decisions about the goals and objectives to be achieved;

- become more aware of stresses and strains generated or imposed;

- choose from a range of possible activities and methods;

- become involved in active planning and problem solving;

- choose how, when and where he or she practises and performs;

- have optimal preparation for physical and mental demands;

- take responsibility for his or her own motivation and enthusiasm;

- become more aware of own abilities and needs;

- decide who they wish to or can involve in their activities;

- relate their learning to real, everyday and personalised goals;

- reduce anxiety through positivity and quantity of experience;

- be able to develop their own 'action plans' to combat physical problems.

Enablers and learning support assistants

These days personal welfare and learning support are generally seen as two parts of the same activity. Outside schools, helpers are sometimes called 'enablers' because their role is not limited to the 'welfare' of a person but encompasses all aspects of a person's life. After all, if we are to follow the principles being outlined in this chapter, *the person with a disability or medical condition should be the one who decides what kind of assistance is needed and when.* It should not be defined by the demarcations or limits of a 'role' decided arbitrarily and enshrined in job descriptions. This is denying choice and opportunity unnecessarily. Pupils with disabilities or medical conditions should not feel that they are a burden. There should be adequate staff who are trained and paid to fulfil an important role in maintaining choice, opportunity and learning for the pupil. But more important than this, it should be a job that they have chosen to do and enjoy. *Often a learning support assistant will become an advocate for a pupil with a disability* who may, for example, need more time to communicate effectively, or to complete the work set. A learning support assistant will often be able to *keep the teacher briefed about day-to-day matters* and it is important that the class or subject teacher is confident about and accepting of this relationship. A learning support assistant will be *the vital mediator between the pupil they are supporting and the work that is planned* and given to the pupil. Care needs to be taken to support sensitively and with due regard to the pupil's growing independence.

Choice and opportunity are critical to a pupil's growth and learning abilities. Good listening skills, flexibility and the confidence to stay in the background (i.e. not intervene) sometimes, are crucial for a pupil to become a fully participating and included member of the class or learning group. Often the learning support assistant needs to work with other pupils and help with general class activities or preparation, so becoming less clearly identified with one pupil. *This will help to prevent stigma and the isolation of the pupil from the rest of the class.* It is a role and a responsibility that demands flexibility and creativity as well as knowledge and skill. The class or subject teacher has the overall responsibility for planning and organising the schemes of work, the IEP and specific differentiated activities for the pupil. The *learning support assistant has the task of supporting and facilitating a pupil (or pupils) in the activities planned.* It is often very effective for the learning support assistant to plan and implement specific activities within a scheme of work. An effective working relationship is a partnership in which the class or subject teacher guides and monitors so that the tasks are clearly related to the direction of overall development in that area or subject and to the pupil's own individual needs. *The quality of the relationships between teacher, support assistant and pupil will have a tremendous impact on the learning and progress.* Open, honest and unfettered relationships will have a major, positive effect on the quality of life and learning of pupils with disabilities, both in the classroom and in the school generally.

Moving, lifting and physical assistance

As very young pupils grow they want to move independently and some will object to being carried. A wheelchair gives some independence and young children will also want to use whatever abilities or potential they have to position and move themselves. They will want to take responsibility for their own movement and for their own posture unless they have been taught to be passive. This may have happened either through over-protectiveness or because there has been too little time to allow for physical problem solving. There must be a balanced and realistic view of what can be done. The experience of being lifted or even hoisted above the ground is one that should be considered carefully. It is not pleasant. It is important that in the training for lifting and handling a good deal of consideration is given to how the person being lifted feels and what is the safest and most secure way for them. Again, when it is necessary to lift or handle, *guidance should come from the pupil or student about the acceptability of different ways* and it should be discussed.

The aspect most often concentrated on is the potential for back strain on the part of carers and enablers. This is important and is sometimes due to inefficient movement, lack of training and lack of proper conditioning. There are also particular health and safety conditions about the weights to be lifted by one or by two people together. The reality of the situation is that these are sometimes stretched because of shortages of staff or lack of time. It is important that these are regularly reviewed and kept in mind, both for the health of the carer or helper and for the safety and security or peace of mind of the person who has a disability. Where lifting occurs, the school should have a policy to cover this aspect of the work and there should be some training on offer. Enablers or support assistants and teachers should be aware of this and of the policy.

Medication and self-management

Pupils with medical conditions may need to manage their own medication or may need to have access to medication during the day. A pupil may have a severe allergy, such as anaphylaxis, where the pupil's involvement is vital in order to make sure that there is no contact with or ingestion of certain substances, foods or chemicals. No school can supervise totally and it would not be fitting in an educational environment to restrict a pupil to the extent that they were not taking any responsibility for themselves, and *hence not learning anything*. In these circumstances it is again important that pupils are involved in the planning and implementation of any strategies or approaches to dealing with medical needs. There are many examples, such as in epilepsy, diabetes or asthma, where it is in the pupil's best interests to learn about and manage the consequences of these illnesses. This should be possible in conjunction with medical and health advice from the school medical service, school nurses and other health professionals.

Summary points (physical disabilities)

A pupil's physical disabilities may be the result of an illness or injury, which might have short- or long-term consequences, or may arise from a congenital condition. Such difficulties may, without action by the school or LEA, limit access to the full curriculum. Some children with physical disabilities may also have sensory problems and learning difficulties.

(DfE 1994, p. 61)

- Pupils with physical disabilities cover the range of ability found in mainstream schools. Additional perceptual or sensory difficulties do not imply any measure of capability or understanding, although these may be additional learning difficulties.

- It is necessary to understand some of the underlying reasons for physical disabilities and their impact upon daily functioning in order to make environmental adjustments and then set appropriate targets and monitor progress.

- The whole of the curriculum and organisation of the school must contribute towards the social, physical and environmental adjustments necessary to include pupils with physical disabilities.

- Aids and adaptations to the physical environment and technology (complex or simple) should be seen as an immediate means to get access to the learning and social environment.

- Access alone is not sufficient; including pupils means adjusting any rigid adherence to existing or inflexible attitudes and approaches, and developing strategies to promote longer-term academic, personal and social development.

- Reasonable adjustments to institutional practices (including attitudes and procedures) are as important as individual targets; it is therefore advisable to:

  institute regular joint reviews with staff involved;
  ensure that all staff implement policies (e.g. equality of opportunity, differentiation, inclusion, etc.).

- Acting to develop skills, knowledge and understanding, beliefs and positive feelings will have a greater impact on pupil progress in the long run than focusing exclusively on individual limitations or problems.

- Directing attention to specific conforming behaviours or unrealistic notions of independence or 'normal' function can damage the feeling of competence and confidence with consequent lowering of self-esteem.

- If targets are not *embedded* within the context of a curriculum then medium- and longer-term progress will not be monitored.

- The individual pupil will develop academically and socially if they are involved in negotiating their targets and are taught appropriately and if progress is measured using adjustments and flexibility.

- A distinction needs to be made between the management of a pupil (teacher target) and the setting of relevant learning objectives (pupil targets). For example, 'regular physiotherapy' is a teacher/adult target. 'Being able to balance on the bench' (like the others . . .) may be a pupil target.

Summary points (medical conditions)

Some medical conditions may, if appropriate action is not taken, have a significant impact on the pupil's academic attainment and/or may give rise to emotional and behavioural difficulties. Some of the commonest medical conditions are likely to be congenital heart disease, epilepsy, asthma, cystic fibrosis, haemophilia, sickle cell anaemia, diabetes, renal failure, eczema, rheumatoid disorders, and leukaemia and childhood cancers.

(DfE 1994, p. 67)

- Pupils with medical conditions cover the range of ability found in mainstream schools.

- It may be necessary to understand some of the underlying reasons for a pupil's medical condition(s) in order to adjust their timetable, schemes of work or learning environment so as to set appropriate targets and monitor progress.

- The whole of the curriculum and organisation of the school must contribute towards the social, emotional and organisational adjustments necessary to ensure welcome continuity and maintenance of academic progress for the pupil.

- Procedures for flexible or additional delivery, medication, therapy or treatments in school should be seen as a means of maintaining access to the academic and social environment of the school, for that pupil (not as an irritating extra 'chore').

- Access to academic continuity means giving the pupil time and the right environment to adjust to radical changes in their life or to radical disruptions to their normal educational routines. Rigid adherence to existing or inflexible approaches can cause significant emotional problems for some pupils.

- Reasonable adjustments to institutional practices (including attitudes and procedures) are as important as individual targets; it is therefore advisable to:

  institute regular joint reviews with staff involved;
  ensure that all staff implement policies (e.g. equality of opportunity, differentiation, inclusion, administration of medicines, etc.).

- Acting to develop skills, knowledge and understanding, beliefs and positive feelings will have a great impact on pupil progress in the long run, raising self-esteem and developing confidence.

- Directing attention to specific conforming behaviours or unrealistic expectations for increased progress ('catching up') or emphasising 'missed time' can damage the feeling of competence and confidence from the start with consequent lowering of self-esteem.

- If targets are not *embedded* within the context of a curriculum and prioritised realistically (and meaningfully with the pupil) then medium- and longer-term progress will not be monitored effectively.

- The individual pupil will develop academically and socially if they are involved in negotiating their targets and are taught appropriately and if progress is measured using adjustments and flexibility.

- A distinction needs to be made between the management of a pupil (teacher target) and the setting of relevant learning objectives (pupil targets). A teacher target might be 'to fill in the missed content in [say] maths . . .'. A pupil target might be 'to understand and be able to use fractions – half, quarter and tenths . . .'. Pupils will not necessarily 'own' teacher targets.

Involving the learner: Institutional self-review

Regular schools with this inclusive orientation are the most effective means of combating discriminatory attitudes, creating welcoming communities, building an inclusive society and achieving education for all; moreover, they provide an effective education to the majority of children and improve the efficiency and ultimately the cost-effectiveness of the entire education system.

(UNESCO Salamanca Statement 1994)

Organising required adjustments to the (National) Curriculum

Group review and planning for subject teachers or heads of departments

Take one pupil who has additional needs in terms of either a physical disability or a medical condition. Take each subject in turn (perhaps limiting yourself to a specific Attainment Target (AT) in each subject), discuss your 'case-study' as a group and then demonstrate or describe how you would, in this case (Table 18).

How do we . . .	Classroom activities and support	Environment, aids and adaptations	School processes and procedures
. . . make the learning experiences *relevant* to the learner?			
. . . give the pupil *access* as an active participant			
. . . show how *cross-curricular skills* are relevant to this AT and the learning process involved?			
. . . achieve *balance* between the demands of the National Curriculum and the learner's personal or additional needs and abilities?			
. . . cater for *progression* in the particular skills, concepts and understanding involved?			
For example: how do we . . . in SCIENCE . . . AT1 Investigate changes to materials . . .	**Classroom activities and support**	**Environment, aids and adaptations**	**School processes and procedures**
. . . make the learning experiences *relevant* to the learner?	Involve the learner as part of a group collecting information from the rubbish pile set up outside the building . . .	Database for recording set up on class/department computer. Able to print and share laptop records with others or contribute to class records.	School computer system interfaces well and easily with laptop computers used by individuals. Pupil is able to make choice to revisit site during free time.
. . . give the pupil *access* as an active participant?	Record information on laptop . . .	Accessible route to the rubbish. Long reach pincers to pick up items.	Pupil able to revisit the rubbish site at other times – to complete work, etc.
. . . and so on			

Table 18

Reviewing the use of communication and alternative methods (Table 19)

	Areas for review	Comment/specific observations
Developmental and individual considerations		
Developmental or functioning level – can the pupil relate to . . .	Objects, miniature objects, coloured pictures, black and white pictures, line drawings, word recognition and reading level?	
Age	Does pupil recognise age-appropriate content? Is pupil selecting age-appropriate content?	
Understanding	Look at *all* indicators of pupil's level of understanding – physical activities/reactions, eye pointing, non-verbal signs, etc. Consider number of goals to reach the required goal, i.e. possibly breaking down the task into smaller components	
Physical requirements	General balance and stable posture while seated Vision and visual processing Hearing and sound processing Shoulder, arm and wrist movement and capability Hand and finger movement – general dexterity Intelligibility of speech – degree of articulation difficulty Advice on possibilities for intelligible speech	
Self-esteem is good . . .?	Seems generally content with self Makes decisions easily and confidently Rarely appears anxious – anxious usually with some reason Participates and is interested – has circle/friends Appears to tackle usual tasks with confidence Laughs or smiles with friends – not overly subdued or isolated Gets over personal and work mistakes within a reasonable time Thinking is flexible – takes new things into account Works successfully with minimal guidance (or is able to guide help successfully)	
Environmental factors		
Attitudes and knowledge of systems	Parents/guardians Teaching staff Therapy staff Carers or care staff Learning support staff	

	Areas for review	Comment/specific observations
Time and support	Only able to use when with enabler/support staff Uses independently in the classroom Uses independently around school (and at home)	
Confident use in social situations	Uses only in classroom for specific activities Uses for most things in the classroom Uses outside the classroom for structured activities Uses nearly all the time for unstructured activities (e.g. play) Uses at home as well as at school	
Developing interaction	Reticent to communicate or interact Enjoys interaction: • with adults • with friends • with new people Always waits and only responds Sometimes initiates interaction: • with adults • with friends • with new people	
Supplementary systems or alternatives to speech		
Additional languages and sign systems	British sign Language (sophisticated with grammar, etc.) Unaided, i.e. manual sign systems which require no support materials Makaton – simplified, no grammar Amerind (pre-symbol level) Signed English	
Aided, i.e. any system which requires support materials		
Simple aided systems	Pictures/lines, drawings Symbols – manipulable (plastic shapes), pictorial, Bliss Rebus, Makaton symbols, Sigsyms Letter/alphabet boards Word boards	
Technical support systems: access via pictures, symbols, letters or words	Visual display, e.g. lightwriter Hard copy print-out, e.g. Cannon Synthetic voice output, e.g. Handivoice Recorded output, e.g. Intro-talker	

Table 19

Involving the learner: Ideas for action

Facilitating meaningful communication

Communication that assists independence is vital in establishing and monitoring what level of help is appropriate for a pupil or student. Figure 4 shows increasing levels of independence and complexity in terms of skill.

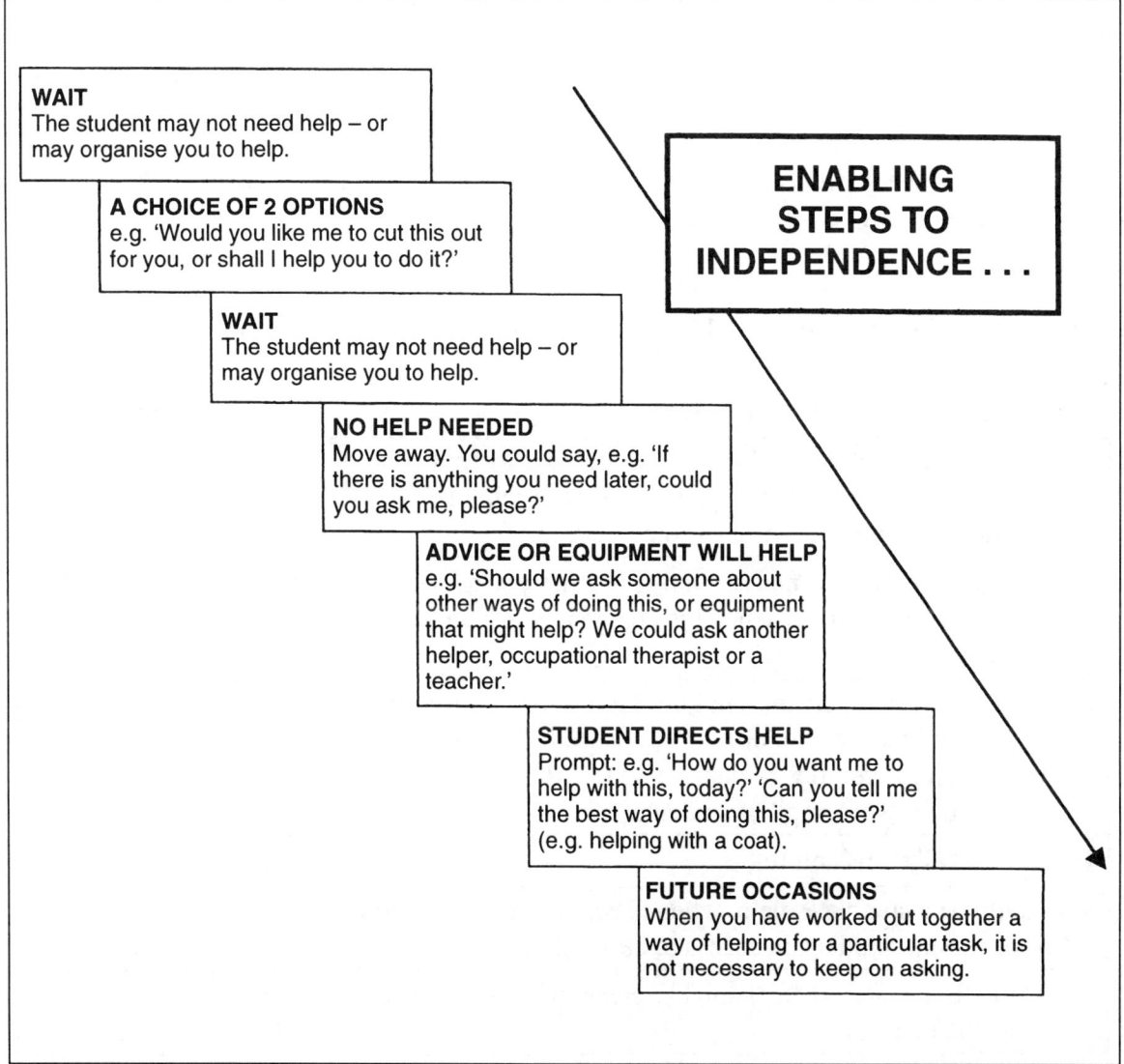

Figure 4

The pupil or student will need to develop increasing independence, in a real sense, through directing their help in more and more sophisticated ways. Figure 4 suggests a progression in communicating his or her needs (courtesy of Webber 1991).

Helpers should:

> - **NOT** assume what help is wanted.
> - **NOT** insist on everything being done independently by the older student with a disability. Students may feel, for example, that for some work that is to be displayed, they would rather ask the helper to do the cutting out, and they will direct how the display is to be arranged – this is their choice.

When working with a student with a disability on any task, it is necessary to explore together the possible ways of helping. The student can then choose for this task, with this helper, on this day, in this context, at this time, how much help she/he wants. It is necessary to be aware that some students may ask for more help than they really need.

If you have already negotiated with the student how she/he wishes to be helped, you only need to check that she/he wants the same help as last time.

Do not assume what kind of help the student wants, as this will take away his/her control and force him/her into a passive role.

What does good learning support mean?

Learning support means assistants . . .	Yes ✔ or No X
✔ need job descriptions and clear roles defined by mutual agreement and understanding, involving the school management and the class or subject teacher;	
✔ need to be well informed (pre-class discussions are of value) to achieve consistency through teamwork and cooperation;	
✔ can help as an amanuensis in note-taking for pupils with significant hand control difficulties; extra help should only be given, however, if it is clearly needed; this should also be discussed with the pupil or student;	
✔ will find IT skills helpful;	
✔ should be available to help, when necessary, with classroom work to help pupils gain access to curriculum;	
✔ facilitate in matters of personal hygiene, basic social needs or medical needs;	
✔ should assist pupil to become independent as possible, depending on the unique needs of a pupil or student;	
✔ (+ *your own additions or ideas . . .*)	

Table 20

Audit of aids and adaptations in use

Alternative input	
Alternative keyboards	
Programmable keyboards	Chording keyboards
Miniature keyboards	On-screen keyboards
Expanded keyboards	
Alternative mouse	
Trackerball	Electric pointer
Joystick	Switch
Glidepoint	Interface devices
Touch screen	Voice recognition
Alternative processing	
Rate enhancement	Menu managers
Maths processors	Braille embossers and translators
Alternative output	
Braille embossers and translators	Closed-circuit television
Screen readers	Reading machines
Speech synthesis	
Software features	
Easy-to-read screens	Auditory cues
Consistency	Visual clues
Intuitive characteristics	Built-in access
Logical labels	Built-in utilities
Instructional choices	Alternatives to a mouse
Graphics	Optional cursors
Friendly documentation	Creation of custom programs
On-screen instructions	
Low-technology aids	
Keyguard	Copy stand
Wrist/arm support	Screen magnifier
Head/mouth/hand stick	Anti-glare filter
Key stickers	Monitor mounts
Keyboard slope	

Table 21

Partnership with parents: Principles

How can parents be involved in IEPs?

The relationships between parents of children with special educational needs and the school which their child is attending has a crucial bearing on the child's educational progress and the effectiveness of any school based action.

Most schools already have effective working relationships with parents, including the parents of children with special educational needs.

School based arrangements should ensure that assessment reflects a sound and comprehensive knowledge of a child and his or her responses to a variety of carefully planned and recorded actions which take account of the wishes, feelings and knowledge of parents at all stages.

Children's progress will be diminished if their parents are not seen as partners in the educational process with unique knowledge and information to impart.

Professional help can seldom be wholly effective unless it builds upon parents' capacity to be involved and unless parents take account of what they say and treat their views and anxieties as intrinsically important.

(Code of Practice 2:28)

The need for empathy and skilled behaviour by those who are at the first point of contact with families who have a disabled child has been emphasised for many years. This is perhaps one of the more sensitive areas for professionals to handle and it is still common for parents, clients and other service users to undergo more negative experiences than necessary. It is generally acknowledged that the first 5 years of a child's life are highly formative.

Involving parents

I am wheelchair bound. My husband is wheelchair bound. Our daughter is wheelchair bound and so is our son. In truth it is only our son who needs the aid of a wheelchair, but it might just as well be the whole family. The effect of having a severely disabled child affects the family unit. Everything is geared around his needs and his disabilities.

(Hirstle 1995)

A pupil with a disability or a long-term medical condition will have had different experiences, even before coming to school. This is true in terms of academic, physical and social experiences. It is also true in terms of the internal relationships within a family, the expectations that they have or can develop and the relationship between the family and the services they may need to access. It is not often that teachers or schools are present at the very first point of contact but they need to be aware of the process that a child and parents may have already been through. A second important area is the wider context of the child and family in the community. Raising public and professional awareness of physical and learning disability is a constant reminder of the great distance we still need to go in this country in fostering realistic and positive attitudes. *Children's early development is integrated* from a young age. This means that movement, hand use and function, speech,

86

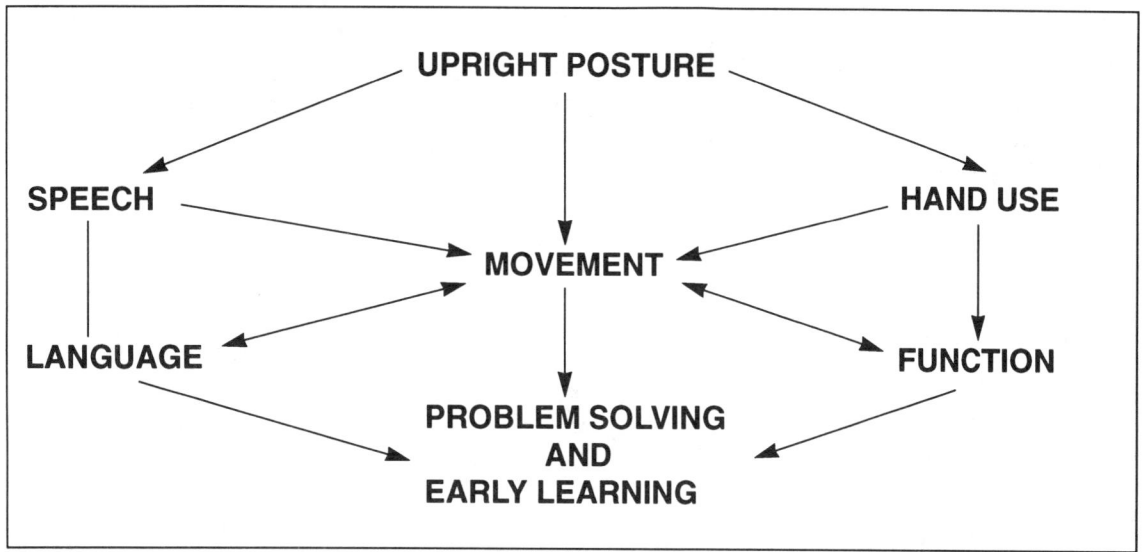

Figure 5

language and problem solving (and other early learning) develop together. The differences for pupils *and* their parents may be apparent in a variety of ways because children's early development is integrated and interdependent (see Figure 5).

Parents often understand the way that a pupil has developed (or not) in one of these areas and, more importantly, the ways in which they might have compensated for or solved some of the problems thrown up by their disability or condition, themselves. This knowledge can be very important in helping to build meaningful strategies to encourage learning and progress.

Quality of life is a somewhat vague term but it is used here to describe the growth of love, security, positive relationships and self-esteem. Parents are the vital centre-point for a child as he or she grows, and children spend more time at home, from birth to 10 years, than at school. *Parents, not having professional status in meetings about a child, are sometimes not listened to sufficiently.* Yet it is they who are the key to providing the foundations for learning, independence, motivation and the ability of the pupil to take risks and actively pursue their goals. This partnership is important in practical terms where there are a number of factors at work:

- a disability or medical condition puts extra demands upon parents ('stresses' mentioned in 'Excellence for all children . . .' (Green Paper, 1998));

- siblings of the disabled child will have had to make adjustments to their own lives;

- parents will most likely have experienced frustration through having to deal with multiple agencies.

It is likely that a pupil with disabilities will have experienced different, but no less caring, experiences within a family as a consequence of the public nature of disability and professional intervention. *Professional interventions*, particularly for pupils born with a disability or condition, start at a young age. Even when the condition is diagnosed in older children, say, at 9 or 10 years old, the pupil can suddenly be subject to a 'confusing soup' of professional interventions and encounters (Cornwall 1997) (see Figure 6).

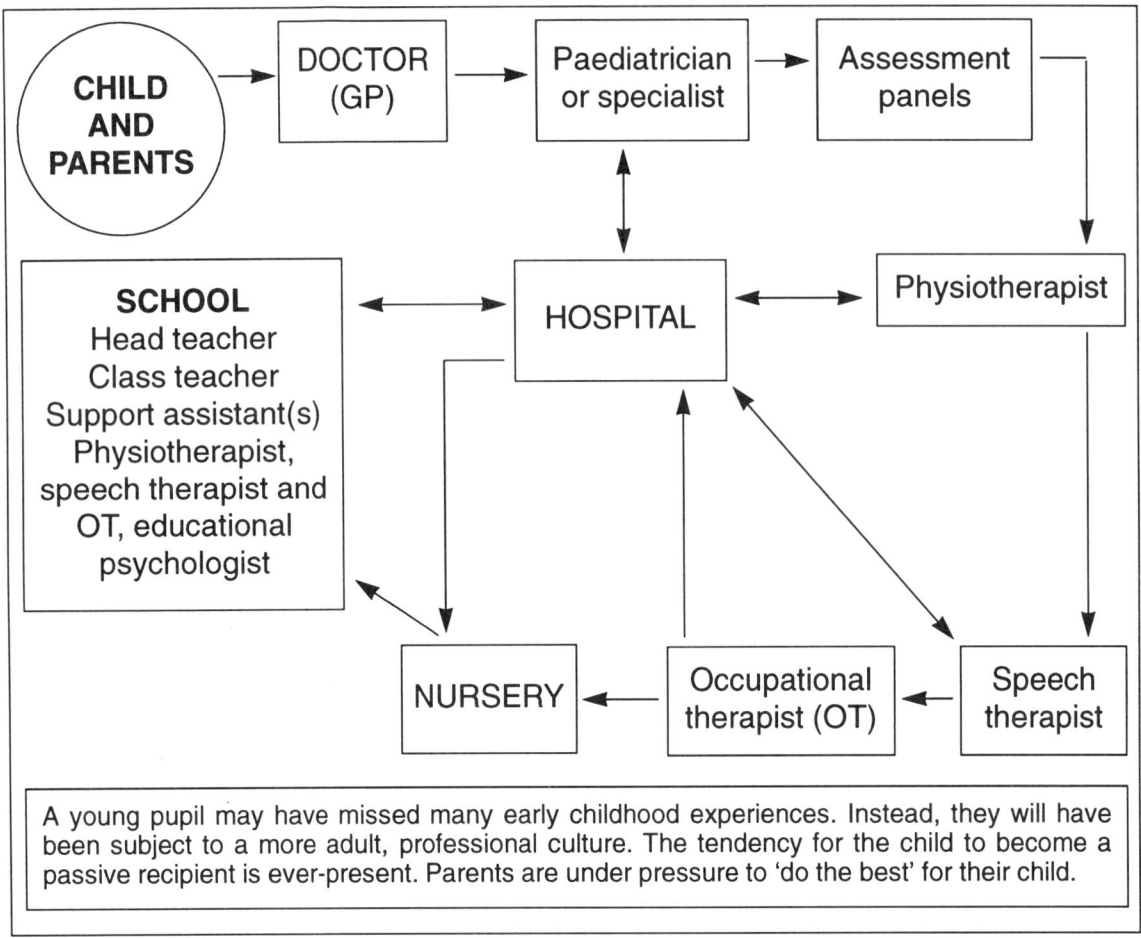

A young pupil may have missed many early childhood experiences. Instead, they will have been subject to a more adult, professional culture. The tendency for the child to become a passive recipient is ever-present. Parents are under pressure to 'do the best' for their child.

Figure 6

Working with professionals

Looking at the equation from a parental perspective can shed a different light on matters. From the parents' viewpoint professional collaboration is a double-edged sword involving:

- *frustration and bewilderment* when dealing with SEN bureaucracy, professionals in different locations, paperwork, appointments galore and sometimes ignorance or misapprehension about the problems they face; and at other times

- *relief and encouragement* when professionals are able to

  understand the nature of their problems;

  recognise the capabilities of their child;

  show a positive, empathetic approach to difficulties encountered;

  assess the situation accurately and give clear responses to their situation (not vague professional proclamations).

Senior managers in schools need to be conscious of whole-staff awareness of the dynamics of parent–professional interaction in relation to disabled pupils (and others labelled as SEN). There are specific consequences for whole-school development, OFSTED requirements and staff development generally. Hornby (1994) proposes a 'model' for working with parents that is effective in using parents' contributions and expertise as well as acknowledging their needs. This model leads to the development of particular skills in listening, communication and even counselling that would be propitious for teachers to become more aware of, if not develop themselves.

Too many professionals assume that all parents view disability as a disaster. Often professionals communicate that this is the case even when parents accept their child in its uniqueness. Sometimes it works the opposite way. In a vain attempt not to upset parents, or to give them false expectations, some professionals over-minimise or dismiss the social consequences, in our society, of being disabled or having an illness.

What does parent partnership mean?

There has been much discussion in recent years about parental choice since the inception of open enrolment. The intentions of the legislation were seemingly to give parents more choice of schools but many parents would argue that the system and the diversification and selectivity of some schools have served to reduce parental choice. Whether they have or not it is clear that parents of children with a physical disability and some with medical conditions in reality have less choice than parents in general. When they do attempt to exercise free choice, say to send their child to their local school, they face many obstacles – not least are the physical environment and the resources needed for any individual pupil with diverse needs. The reality is that many children with disabilities will have to travel some distance, involving a lengthy bus journey, to attend a school that can meet their needs. These are some of the unspoken 'pressures' mentioned in the Government Green Paper 'Excellence for all children . . .' (DfEE 1998).

For teachers, head teachers and schools as a whole, this is an important starting point because it implies that partnership with parents involves listening to, and understanding, parents' experience. One positive spin-off from this approach is that they can learn a great deal about the condition or disability itself. Parents are often experts in their own particular area even though they may feel 'at sea' with it or even incapable in the face of professional expertise. They have an in-depth knowledge, through experience, not only of the condition itself, but also of the consequences (social, emotional and cultural) of that particular condition. Their knowledge and understanding are very often part of the solution when it is unlocked by effective and sensitive partnership.

Parents of young children

There are a number of additional considerations for teachers and learning support staff working with parents of young children, whose experience is fairly recent and who may still be grappling with both the problems caused by the physical disability or medical condition and the problems they have to face in the community. They will inevitably have to cope with an environment that has become more hostile. This happens either unwittingly in the way the community and the environment are planned or sometimes wittingly through prejudice and stereotyped attitudes – of which one is blind pity, another is patronising help and another plain intolerance and impatience.

Self-confidence

We must encourage parents to feel good about their parenting. Having a disabled child can make parents feel inadequate and that their natural skills are not appropriate. In our work we may 'deskill' parents by making them feel that it is necessary to have years of special training before we can help a child, or that their intuitive actions are not worth very much unless they can be justified by specialist knowledge.

The child's family needs to *feel good about their disabled member and about themselves*. If we concentrate all our support on the mother, then the father may feel isolated, unable to help and useless.

The family must also *feel confident about listening to professionals and expert opinion*. It takes confidence to be able to accept advice from others, particularly in personal areas.

Hospital school services

Hospital school services are charged (by the 1993 Education Act) to arrange suitable education for all pupils of compulsory school age who are out of school because of illness or injury. The DfEE Circular 9/94 aims to ensure continuity of provision with a view to the least possible disruption to effective education. It emphasises that the education of these children still remains the responsibility of their main school and is achieved through effective collaboration. If a child is ill or additional educational support is required, parents will need to be referred to, or work with, the education welfare service, the GP, the hospital consultant and the hospital school service in their particular area. A pupil may qualify for direct support from the hospital school service in their area if his/her education is disrupted because of:

- an illness or injury keeping the pupil away from school during recovery (for example, a broken limb or recovery from an operation or a road traffic accident);

- an illness or injury requiring regular hospital attendance (for example, cystic fibrosis, asthma, epilepsy or haemophilia);

- a mental illness requiring therapeutic support and for which parents are actively seeking help (for example, depression, anxiety or anorexia).

A pupil may receive support in one or more of the following ways:

- tuition in hospital;

- tuition in the home;

- tuition in a group in a day centre;

- day provision in a hospital school.

The consequence of this service, while maintaining effective education for the pupil, is to put a great deal of pressure on parents in attending meetings, transporting the pupil to and from hospital for treatment, visiting in hospital and so on. It may be that by the time the pupil is well again and coming back into the main(stream) school, the parents will be exhausted. Great care needs to be taken to plan (or have strategies and plans ready) for welcoming such pupils (and their parents) back to school.

Parents of school-aged children

The needs of the family remain similar. However, perhaps there are a few new areas for consideration in the interface between home and school. Some would see these as skills that parents need to acquire; others more of a contract between home and school. There is no doubt that both teachers (with counselling, listening and collaborative skills) and parents need to have a range of skills or understanding for the interface to work more successfully. Here are some tentative examples of areas for consideration.

- Parents need to understand the school's approach and the way in which the school conceives its programme, the opportunities for the pupil and a longer-term vision for the pupil's development.

- It is good if the parents can contribute to or follow some school programmes for their child, e.g. some particular or individual aspects that they would be best at (some aspect of personal development – independence in dressing, etc.).

- Parents can contribute greatly to the development of specific communication or physical skills for a disabled child and to maintaining self-esteem and confidence in a child who has an illness and misses school, for example.

- Teachers need to understand the stresses and strains of parenthood and this should be reciprocated by some understanding of potential emotional responses of staff – particularly with children whose disabilities or illnesses are severe.

Parents and the law

The Code of Practice (1994) emphasises strongly the role of parents as partners with their child's school. Not only should they be informed of arrangements in school but also their views should be incorporated in the assessment of their child and all subsequent reviews (2.33). The involvement of the pupils themselves should be sought and recorded, especially when transition reviews or post-school arrangements are being made (6.59). Head teachers consider that the Code of Practice has helped to improve contacts with parents. They report that there are more contacts and increased correspondence (Clutterbuck and Skeet 1998). However, most schools merely keep records of parental contacts rather than details of the issues raised by parents or points discussed. A school's recording of the outcomes of a discussion with parents can become very useful in situations where pupils are later considered for statutory assessment; it can form an important component of the school's portfolio of evidence to show how they have helped the child at earlier stages of the Code of Practice. Recent research (Clutterbuck and Skeet 1998) has thrown up some interesting insights into the way that the Code of Practice and IEPs have affected the partnership between schools and parents.

- Most schools are conscious that the way they inform parents of their child's progress could be improved and that *parental involvement in the review of IEPs* is often nominal.

- Parents are often encouraged to attend the review but there is *great variation in parental response*.

- Primary school links with parents are more effective than those in secondary schools.

- Some schools, especially primary schools, *alert parents to their concerns about their child's progress at Stage 1* while others involve parents only from Stage 2 onwards.

- Many schools have procedures for consulting parents regularly but if parents do not attend the review meetings they are not necessarily informed of the outcome.

- *Annual reviews for pupils with statements* result in much higher parental attendance, and more schools are incorporating parental views in the documents that are subsequently sent to the LEA.

- Parental involvement at each stage is seen as very time-consuming for SENCOs and other SEN staff. *It is very expensive if staff cover is provided* to release class teachers and SENCOs for every review meeting, and there are *particular problems with 'hard to reach' families*.

- Some schools, however, have worked very successfully with parents and are involving them at all stages of identification and provision.

- *Pupils are still seldom involved in the development of their IEPs or in reviews.*

- Staff admit that *many parents are confused by the terms* 'review', 'register', 'statement', etc. Schools need to be much clearer in their brochures, guidance and annual reports for parents and to define the terms they use.

- *Named persons, as well as parent partnership schemes, have had relatively little impact* on the schools' SEN practices and policies in this survey. Information about local parent partnership schemes has often not been passed to schools, and as a consequence many schools know very little about these schemes and are therefore unable to inform parents.

Summary points

- Parental involvement in a child's IEP is vital. It is not an intrusion into a school's procedures and processes in response to special needs nor can it become an afterthought once procedures are put in place.

- Parents have a right to be informed about and involved in the decision making regarding their child. The insights and opinions of parents are at least as valid as those of professionals involved in the IEP.

- The relationship that a parent of a child has with the school will be an extension and elaboration of existing good policy and practice for parental partnership with the school.

- Having a child with a physical disability or medical condition invariably causes extra stress and worry as well as imposing additional responsibilities on the parent.

- Parents, particularly those who are themselves *anxious, may find it easier to work with staff concerned on a focused impersonal task* than engage in a discussion about 'the condition of your child'.

- The IEP provides a *focus* for collaborative planning; filling in the plan enables 'joint attention' with parents to be established at an early point in the meeting.

- The parents are asked to state what worries them about their child ('concerns'). This 'concern' *focus allows parents to give their perspective initially* rather than adopting a defensive role.

- 'Agreeing targets' does provide a framework for collaborative working. Some SENCOs have suggested that *if three targets are to be selected then at least one should be chosen by the parents.*

- Parents are in a unique position to suggest which strategies would work for their child. This places them in an *appropriate position as providers of information* to support school planning rather than receivers of 'what we are going to do . . .'.

- The fact that the IEP is a 'planning' and not a reporting document affords the opportunity for the SENCO, the class teacher or outside agencies *to suggest to parents what strategies might be used for meeting targets.*

- The need to review IEPs on a regular basis means that *parents can be kept informed* as part of an on-going process – not on a 'crisis' basis.

- The IEP provides an opportunity *for parents to work with their child on agreed targets.* This is in contrast to plans which involve adults 'talking about' the child and making plans 'for' and not 'with' them.

- SEN pupils are often subjected to many 'assessments' and advice. Parents can become confused by this. As *effort by all concerned in the IEP is focused towards the development and achievement of targets* this can result in parents receiving more coordinated support than they might normally experience.

Partnership with parents: Institutional self-review

What could be done to improve partnership with parents and the quality of provision for pupils with medical conditions or physical disabilities (see Table 22)?

(The third column contains comments from teachers and parents recorded during joint workshops looking at partnership issues – 1997.)

Partnerships in . . .	Some existing and new strategies	Problems/opportunities . . . comments from teachers and parents
Early intervention	*Counselling and support* for parents right from the start *Medical reports* – have to be a central base for information from many sources (e.g. 14 different specialists) *Key person/professional* needs to coordinate with the various professional groups (or advocate for child/parents) *Voluntary support groups* can provide a focus and outlet for parent's views	*Numbers of children* involved Identification and assessment for provision of resources – the process needs to be speeded up radically Parents feel that one hurdle to overcome is the one 'belief' – *believing their child's need is 'real'* *Time is important*; we see huge benefits coming from meetings, etc., but in reality the frequency of meetings can be low
Support to the family	To develop an awareness of the child's needs To develop the confidence to treat the child as 'normally' as possible	Teachers need to realise *how significant each child is* Not all professionals understand – transfer from school to school or from services to service, etc. Emotional support Parents *do all* have expertise to offer – some parents do not realise this Parents need to take social opportunities Parents who don't want to come
Agency support	Needs of child and family to be accurately identified Consistent and coordinated strategies by all agencies Effective interagency dialogue Persistence by outsiders in challenging situations Encouragement of self-actualisation of child with disability Importance of accurate record keeping	*Being available* – time and availability of teacher or parent 'Experts' often advise parents as to what is best for their child Money is often the final deciding factor Drawing upon each other's expertise give mutual support Professionals need to listen and not make assumptions Too many helpful hints from professionals Lack of understanding Support groups More liaison between parents and carers Mutual support for both parents and professionals

Partnerships in . . .	Some existing and new strategies	Problems/opportunities . . . comments from teachers and parents
Education	Adequate and regular monitoring and adjustment of provision Adequate and regular communication between family and school Staff education and training Peer education and raising awareness of disability and illness issues SEN seen as part of whole-school policy	Also, parents may feel that schools can blame them in some way for the child's problem – this can be intimidating ✓ League tables and selection ✓ Parents' expectations cannot always be met ✓ Time-shares with other children in the class ✓ Human resources, materials, space, money ✓ Classroom assistants – not always trained; too much responsibility in implementing the programme ✓ Communication between parents and school ✓ Accessibility – schools are not always welcoming ✓ Social gatherings, consultation evenings ✓ Teachers/providers need to listen more to parental needs and be more open with criticism ✓ Parents need to go to parents' evenings ✓ Not always able to be honest . . . worried about upsetting school ✓ Code of Practice: issues and steps involved need to be more clearly defined
Resources	Improve physical problems *now* Appropriate provision – not lip service	Parent power: ✓ Support ✓ Resources, etc. Parents have a lifetime of knowledge about their child Parents have details of problems
Disability awareness	National awareness and education programme Staff education and training Peer education and raising awareness of disability and illness issues	Enables a better learning environment for all children Classroom teachers' expertise increases Greater understanding of whole child

Table 22

Training: Principles

Staff development is a very effective way of engaging in a mutual process of change for staff, pupils and management. It provides the space to consider what is going on, what the goals are and who holds what opinions and views. It is a time of sharing, considering, discussion, argument and even conflict. During this time, people have the opportunity to make an assessment of the skills they feel they have and the skills and knowledge they feel they need to improve and practise. It is important that people do not feel deskilled by new initiatives or changes, all of which are healthy and productive if organised and handled well. It is usually better for an outside consultant to work through some issues and to provide an outside view for the staff.

Schools can also use their own internal resources and expertise. For example, physiotherapists can show teachers how to position pupils and explain how much to expect of them in terms of physical effort and stamina. Teachers can appraise physiotherapists of the school's PE curriculum and together they can work out ways of integrating their effort to the benefit of pupils. Speech therapists may be able to help with alternative and augmentative communication and work with teachers on pupils' progress within the English curriculum or on the new literacy initiatives. It is important that learning support or classroom assistants are involved in this kind of consultation and discussion to increase understanding of the pupil's needs and abilities.

The incorporation of an element on *awareness about physical or movement disability* might be part of the school's social education programme for all pupils. It should not just be relegated to 'health education' as a classification of syndromes, diseases or medical problems. This is insulting to disabled students and is of little practical value in an educational and social setting. One school in Kent enabled its disabled pupils to develop a booklet for all the pupils in the school giving their point of view and what they felt could be of help in their daily school life.

One of the most effective ways to raise awareness in both staff and pupils is to have the many elements of disability awareness present in the books, materials, resources and information about the school. To have all aspects reflected throughout the curriculum and involve ALL pupils in projects that have a direct bearing on inclusion and access are valuable training initiatives in themselves.

There are a variety of ways in which *an external consultant can work with your school* to support the school's growth and development and to generate change or review. The table on p. 96 is a brief summary and incorporates a broad view of training strategies for staff development (intervention strategies applied by Scope – Education and Management Consultants, in working with schools and LEAs on whole-school and staff development; adapted from Schmuck and Miles 1971 and Francis 1987).

For pupils with physical disabilities or medical conditions, there are areas of knowledge and understanding that define the content of training and staff development initiatives. It is important to note that the starting point of this book and of work with staff in this area is an ethical one, based upon rights and issues of disability and illness in our society. However, this is not sufficient on its own and needs to be accompanied by a clear outline of the specific areas of knowledge and understanding that will back up good teaching skills in providing for this group of children and young people in schools. The following sections provide a very basic outline of some of the important areas for training and staff development.

Direct training or education would involve a variety of activities including lectures, practical exercises, discussion groups, simulations, workshops, buzz groups and T-groups.
Process consultation. This type of activity concentrates on observing on-going processes or activities (such as teaching or group interactions) and providing feedback that is either formally structured as part of a training programme or informal to groups or individuals in the school.
Confrontation or challenge. In bringing together units, groups or individuals that have a poor history of communication the consultant or trainer aims to facilitate changes in outlook or in attitudes. Sometimes these are measurable – often they are not. Sometimes it is necessary to challenge existing thinking or systems in order for them to be developed further or established if they prove good.
Data feedback. This is an objective approach that involves the systematic collection of information and in-school or comparative data which are reported back to the school or service in such a way as to highlight development needs or facilitate change.
Making plans, developing strategies and setting goals. Dealing with planning and goal setting based on a view of the whole school or service system. Working with groups within staff to develop strategies based around a central vision or ethos.
Organisation developmental tasks and working groups. Linking training to specific developmental tasks both for individuals and for the system, school or service as a whole. *Ad hoc* groups or systematic structures evolve or are set up to provide structure for solving problems and carrying out plans.
Techno-structure activity. Focusing on structural factors, work flow and means of accomplishing tasks. Looking at working conditions, management structures, people problems and strengths and human resource factors. Also providing specialist input (or technical expertise) on specific subjects.

Team building and collaborative skills

People are the most important resource in any organisation. For example:

- they control all other available resources;
- they are 'non-finite' (although not infinite);
- they are the source of enthusiasm, motivation and energy.

Collaborative skills and effective teamwork are particularly important for those in a leadership position, whether this is in the school's management team, as a coordinator or as a teacher with specialist knowledge. Effective provision for pupils with additional needs, whether physical, medical or in other areas of SEN, depends largely on the cooperation and teamwork involved.

Some of these skills are listed in Table 26, followed by broader considerations of the skills and characteristics of an effective 'enabler'. These all contribute to the effectiveness of teamwork within a school and to the school's ability to collaborate effectively with outside services and agencies.

Effective training and staff development will take the head teacher and staff through some complex issues and will require the learning of new skills. Often, too little time is allocated to make important changes. A combination of professional and organisational skills will be used by all staff, whether a 'key person' with special responsibilities or a learning support assistant with responsibility for one pupil or student.

Classroom assistant's training – some issues

Primary teaching is a complex activity and the roles of teachers are not always clear. One recommendation is that teachers spend more time working with small groups of children while

Professional skills	Professional knowledge
Evaluating materials	Implications of disability and medical needs
Task analysis	Classroom techniques
Matching pupil to task	Teaching techniques and approaches
Objective setting	Developmental stages
Curriculum modifications	Materials that are effective
Devising/sustaining work programmes	Concepts that are appropriate
Adapting resources	Support structures – in class and school
Assessment/records	Support agencies – and access to them
Classroom modifications	Legislation and ethics
Organisational skills	**Organisational knowledge**
Running a meeting	How organisations work
'Advisory' skills (e.g. 'collaborative' as above)	Group dynamics
In-service skills (e.g. presentational)	Negotiating frameworks
Co-teaching skills	Interprofessional barriers
Managing resources and timetable	Liaison with outside agencies
Problem solving techniques	Organisational types or structures
Discussion and liaison skills	

Table 26

the classroom assistant adopts a monitoring role. If learning is enhanced by knowledge of pedagogy and curriculum content, then this should be used to full capacity by the teacher in the role of individual supporter. The other roles of classroom management could be given to classroom assistants, many of whom are already developing such skills. Teachers may feel that this will erode their authority over the class and blur the lines of responsibility for safety and control. If team members and, perhaps most importantly, the children understand the different adult roles during activities, this should enhance the specialised teaching strategies of highly trained and skilled teachers and provide a more clearly defined role for classroom assistants.

There are still many issues surrounding classroom assistants, their training, employment and deployment. The crucial issue is the definition of 'teaching' and whether it is possible to produce what might be described as 'partial' teachers (given that courses often replicate the first year of an undergraduate initial training degree).

- Are there elements of 'teaching' that are considered appropriate for a support worker to do under the guidance of a qualified teacher?

- The level of functioning that can be expected of classroom assistants with differential training requires clarification.

- Questions also need to be raised as to the feasibility and desirability of extending the role as a panacea for increasing class sizes.

- Reasons for the employment and deployment of classroom assistants warrant much sharper debate.

The Government's latest proclamations, through the Teacher Training Agency, suggest that more emphasis will be placed on developing the role of the classroom assistant. Learning support assistants, special assistants, classroom assistants are doing much valuable work, and in the USA, they are now called 'para-educators'. However, it remains to be seen whether there will be a genuine attempt to provide additional resources in order to reduce class sizes, which is the major impediment to effective inclusive education, or whether, as the research above suggests, it will be used as a panacea for ever-increasing class sizes.

Summary points

- There should be a process of constant review, and training initiatives, both in initial teacher training and in continuing professional development, in the basic qualities of good teaching, managing a classroom, equality of opportunity, disability and human rights, effective communication and forming positive relationships. These are some of the basic conditions that will encourage inclusion and participation.

- Continuing professional development should also include interpersonal skills, physical and social development in the early years, incorporating communication (including alternative and augmentative communication), language and literacy into programmes and continuing detailed training in matching education to particular individual needs.

- Teachers and other staff need substantial training in order to be able to separate medical advice, therapeutic contributions to pupils' development, access issues and the planning of a full educational and academic programme (including an IEP).

- All staff should have training in early years development in order to recognise where a pupil has been, or is being, denied access to good educational experience. They also need to understand the integrated nature of early years development where experiences are built upon.

- Collaborating and working alongside a range of other professionals and with parents and families is an important part of this work. All staff need continuing training in contributing to the team or joint effort – training in teamwork skills to implement IEPs.

- Appropriate staff with 'key worker' roles, monitoring or coordinating responsibilities, will need training in the organisational skills of monitoring and coordination to ensure the quality of provision and planning and to advocate for an individual.

- Children need to feel they are learning, and feedback from teachers which is focused and sustaining will also motivate and enhance pupils' self-esteem. Training for enhanced interpersonal skills as well as classroom management is important and training in goal setting or target setting may provide more focused and accurate feedback to pupils.

- Some pupils will require assistance with their communication and may use alternative or augmentative systems (some complex and technological, some not complex at all). Teachers need to be aware of the principles of good communication, which have nothing to do with technology but can be applied to all communication situations.

- Teachers will, of necessity, be working with pupils who are using information (e.g. computers, communicators) or medical (e.g. drugs, injections) technologies. It is important that training enables teachers to be aware of the sources of technical advice and practical support. They also need to be able to recognise potential problems and refer these to the appropriate sources.

- Full use of other professional and specialist expertise (e.g. therapies, medical input, hospital school services, counselling, equality of opportunity, disability rights) should be made in developing effective training programmes for all staff.

- Ideally, joint training initiatives should develop between disciplines and professions working alongside pupils with physical disabilities and medical conditions.

- Inclusion and equality of opportunity are the underpinning principles that guide strategies and approaches related to IEP planning. Teachers and senior managers should have the opportunity to explore these issues in principle and then develop an ethos of inclusion based upon practical school-based strategies and approaches.

Training: Institutional self-review

Generating a view of training needs . . .

This is not a simple matter and it could be said to be a requirement of *all of the training undertaken in a school*, whether it is to develop security in subject knowledge, to understand more about physical disabilities, medical conditions and inclusion or to have a direct impact on classroom practice. Table 23 suggests some examples of specific areas for review. It is a starting point for discussion by staff on human rights and inclusion, to check the consensus on disability and inclusion issues. It will generate many initial issues, but it is not exhaustive and experiences will suggest many more.

Statement about inclusion	Agree/ disagree	Comment
All children have the right to learn and grow together in school.		
Children should not be devalued or discriminated against by being sent away because of their disability or condition.		
Special schools have additional resources for children with additional needs.		
Children do not need to be protected from each other or from disability/illness issues.		
There are no legitimate reasons to separate children for their education. Children belong together – with advantages and benefits for everybody.		
Research shows children do better, academically and socially, in inclusive settings.		
There is no teaching or care in a segregated school that cannot take place in an ordinary school.		
Special education is about staff expertise and this is more concentrated in a special environment.		
Given commitment and support, inclusion is a more efficient use of educational resources.		
Segregation teaches children to be fearful and ignorant and breeds prejudice.		
All children need a mainstream education that will help them develop relationships and prepare them for life.		
Only inclusion has the potential to reduce fear and promote friendship, respect, understanding and cooperation.		

Table 23

Training: Ideas for action

The skills of teaching tend to be a constant factor, despite the fact that there has been too much 'mystery' and 'myth' associated with special education and the teaching of children with SEN. It is important from the training viewpoint to be clear about the difference between *the knowledge base that guides teachers' actions and overall planning* (e.g. knowledge about disability or about specific medical conditions) and *teaching skills that enable the teacher to organise the learning environment and communicate with children*. These are two distinct things and are both important but it must be said that the teaching skills are what all teachers have in common. Good teachers in mainstream schools, given the opportunity to refer to a new or different body of knowledge to guide their actions, will have the skills to be good teachers in more specialised settings. Figure 7 illustrates this.

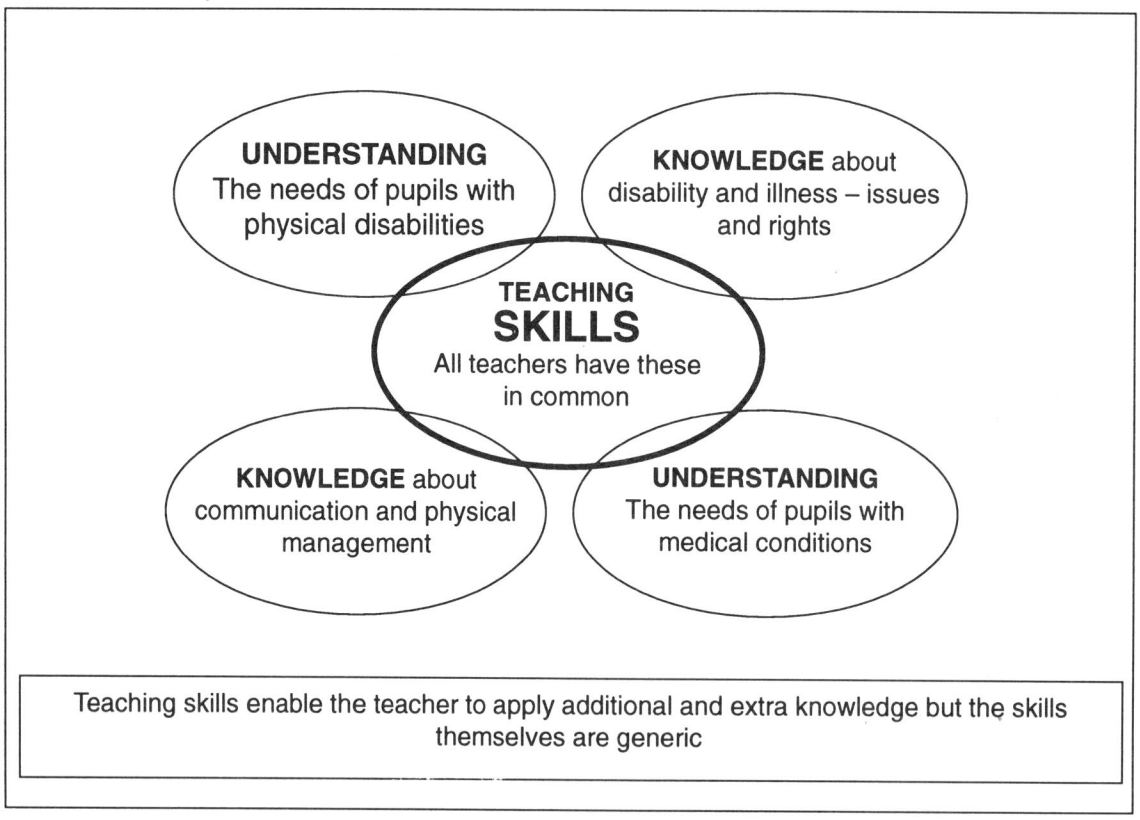

Figure 7

The following table is a summary giving some examples in the third column of more specialist knowledge related to the teacher's skills and actions in teaching. You may wish to fill in or add to the information in the columns – it is by no means exhaustive.

Area of teacher effectiveness	Specific skills and activities involved	Examples: specific knowledge or actions related to disability or medical factors . . . IEP planning . . .
Curriculum planning and preparation	Consider evidence from earlier work and assess the needs of the individual and groups.	School organisation supports this, to alleviate many fears: ● receiver staff should be able to see the pupil at home or at feeder school; ● reciprocally, the pupil should meet receiving staff.
	Take account of pupils' statements and the objectives set at their last reviews.	As much pupil history must be accumulated as possible from parents and consistently between teachers.
	Indicate that activities are matched to ability and age.	Staff should be aware of the ways and at what level the pupil: ● communicates verbally/non-verbally; ● moves, sits and handles objects (physical needs); ● records and uses written work.
	Have clear activity aims with: ● suitable introduction; ● planned development of activity; ● extension/support ideas (including homework where appropriate).	For example, talking books can aid learning for pupils who are physically exhausted by traditional methods of reading. Presenting material in small segments can often make the difference between independent learning and time-consuming one-to-one tutoring.
	Ensure that all students have access to the National Curriculum for a reasonable time, e.g. that the appropriate programmes of study are delivered and all relevant attainment targets met unless alternative modifications have been agreed at the annual review.	Physical adaptations should be decided. Is it, for instance, necessary to install or arrange (a) special toileting facilities, (b) ramps, (c) grab rails, (d) a lift (or modification in classroom usage), (e) safe storage space for crutches, etc. within reach of users? Freedom of movement, whether assisted or independent, is of greatest importance. Most physically disabled pupils are able to take part in some form of physical education. A programme may require specialist help to begin with.
	Ensure that the special needs of the children as set out in their statements and review objectives are met through an appropriately differentiated curriculum which is related to their needs and ability.	Any special emergency procedures should be anticipated and made known to the staff concerned. Help, support and advice from specialist personnel should be encouraged, for example from specialist teachers, physiotherapists and speech therapists.
	Reflect a curriculum which is broad, balanced, relevant and differentiated and which has regard to equal opportunities.	In-service training is essential to acquaint staff with the disability question, the most common disabling conditions and the psycho-physical and academic factors associated with them and also to convince staff that beyond an unattractive body lies a real child who thinks and acts like other children.
	Create schemes of work which are readily available for reference.	Important notices must be within easy sight, perhaps placed lower than normal, particularly if the pupil is wheelchair-bound. Several teachers remarked on the degree of independence this gave pupils, enhancing their feelings of being part of the class.
	Show awareness of the obligation to record and report the personal, educational and social needs of the children.	Teachers must give priority to organising the classroom in such a way that the disabled pupil's social and emotional development, as well as academic progress, is encouraged as much as possible.

Area of teacher effectiveness	Specific skills and activities involved	Examples: specific knowledge or actions related to disability or medical factors . . . IEP planning . . .
	Recognise the need for varied and appropriate use of equipment and resources.	Often, because of disability, the pupil uses muscles with abnormal tone to perform tasks. All available adaptive methods and/or aids must be used in order to increase independence and efficiency of working.
	Ensure the availability of resources.	Teachers should be ready to cope with specialised equipment and be aware of signs that it is not working properly.
	Link activities with department/ school schemes and ensure continuity in the learning process.	The physically disabled pupil may have less energy than a non-disabled one, thus reducing his or her ability to cope with the full school day. The class teacher needs to be alert to signs of fatigue, to provide opportunities for rest and to reduce work volume where necessary.
	Link aspects across the whole curriculum.	Furniture should be arranged in such a way that the pupil can move about freely and see all of the room in its different perspectives. This encourages incidental learning and makes the pupil feel that he or she is part of the class.
	Link recommendations regarding curriculum content for special needs to other areas of the children's programme within school, e.g. independence training, physiotherapy programme.	Class teachers should be prepared to work in the classroom with support staff such as welfare assistants and physiotherapists, and to collaborate with colleagues in order to share information and skills. Physically disabled pupils should have an equal chance to take part in the school's extra-curricular activities. Advance planning may be necessary, particularly if the pupil is taken to school by taxi.
Teaching and Learning Strategies	Learning activities meet the needs of individual children regardless of their special needs, race, colour, gender or ability.	The mobility of the pupil should be fully assessed: how and when physical help will be needed, what physical position and postures are to be encouraged or discouraged and what physiotherapy is necessary. Teachers must be prepared to deal with the asthmatic, epileptic or diabetic pupil in case of emergency – to cope with a seizure, to have sugar available for diabetics, for instance.
	The learning activities, designed to enable children to achieve and develop the aims of the lesson/ activity, are clear in the teacher's mind and are clearly communicated to the children.	Teachers will need to be flexible as to volume (but not quality) of work and the way it is produced.
	Approaches reflect the needs of the children by being sufficiently broad, balanced, relevant and *differentiated* and providing for whole-class, individual and group work.	Classmates should be made familiar with the pupil's disabilities and special needs.
	The teachers' expertise in the subject-matter or activity is sufficient to meet the educational needs of the children.	Some teachers reported very good results from discussing the problem with the class. Such discussions reinforced the pupils' awareness

Area of teacher effectiveness	Specific skills and activities involved	Examples: specific knowledge or actions related to disability or medical factors . . . IEP planning . . .
	Children are involved in/enjoy their own learning, by: • finding their own routes to success; • using their own ideas and questions; • predicting the consequences of their own actions; • thinking for themselves; • evaluating and improving both the processes and product of their work; • recording and presenting their work.	Advice on classroom management should be at hand – for instance on the durability and suitability of certain furniture, since some items are less stable, and on adaptations to help the pupil manage books, pencils and other materials.
	Children are encouraged to: • make rational deductions from experience; • make rational judgements; • develop generalisations about their particular experiences; • communicate, in a variety of forms, their ideas to others; • develop confidence to negotiate the way forward in an activity.	The teacher is ready to organise the classroom to accommodate specialised equipment such as touch talker or wheelchair or ventilator. The pupil is allowed to be as independent as possible. It is important that the teaching space allows the pupil to move around as independently as possible and become an accepted social member of the group. It is recommended that any equipment needed by pupils is as unobtrusive as possible and does not constitute a physical barrier between disabled pupils and their peers.
	The teacher recognises the importance of the following. Start of the lesson or activity: • gaining the children's attention; • the initial instructions; • the initial tasks. During the lesson or activity: • purposeful involvement of the children; • productive involvement of the teacher; • effective transition from one activity to another. End of lesson or activity: • satisfactory conclusion; • appropriate homework when necessary; • departure of the children.	Suitable seating is provided. Physically disabled pupils must have stable, secure seating at the right height and may also need tables so that wheelchairs can get under them. Pupils can outgrow furniture and several teachers remarked on the need to monitor the arrangements. The teacher should be ready to organise the classroom to accommodate specialised equipment such as an electric typewriter or book holders. Some pupils will need additional time in between lessons to get from one place to another.

Table 24 gives a checklist of suggested training areas for staff working with pupils with medical conditions.

Have you covered these areas yet?

Area to be covered in training	✓ or x	Your comments, observations, ideas for action . . .
✓ The legal context and human or ethical issues		
✓ The types of medical conditions encountered and their frequency		
✓ The role of the hospital school services – effective collaboration		
✓ Pupils' short- and longer-term medical and social needs		
✓ Non-prescription medication and social issues		
✓ Health and safety – management and risk assessments		
✓ Pupil's self-management of medication and illness		
✓ Giving and storing medication – access, responsibilities and issues		
✓ Record keeping and emergency procedures		
✓ School trips and sporting activities		
✓ School transport and longer journeys		
✓ Introducing and developing the school policy		

Table 24

References

Bakker, F. *et al.* (1990) *Sport Psychology: Concepts and Applications*. Chitchester. John Wiley & Sons.

Barnes, C. (1991) *Disabled People in Britain and Discrimination: A Case for Anti-discrimination Legislation*. C. Hurst & Co.

Barton, C. (1995) 'Disabling schools and colleges', in Cornwall, J. (ed.) *Choice, Opportunity and Learning: Educating Children and Young People Who Are Physically Disabled*. London: David Fulton Publishers.

Clutterbuck, R. and Skeet, C. (1998) 'Special educational needs: efficient use of resources', *Education Law Monitor* **5**(5), 8–9.

Cornwall, J. (ed.) (1995) *Choice, Opportunity and Learning: Educating Children and Young People Who Are Physically Disabled*. London: David Fulton Publishers.

Cornwall, J. (1997) *Access to Learning: Pupils with Physical Disabilities*. London: David Fulton Publishers.

Cornwall, J. and Tod, J. (1998) *IEPs – Emotional and Behavioural Difficulties*. London: David Fulton Publishers.

DfE (1994) *Code of Practice on the Identification and Assessment of Special Educational Needs*. London: HMSO.

DfEE and Department of Health (1996) *Supporting Pupils with Medical Needs in School*. London: HMSO.

DfEE (1997) *The SENCO Guide*. London: HMSO.

DfEE (1998) 'Excellence for all children (meeting special educational needs) . . .'. London: HMSO.

Fenton, M. and Hughes, P. (1989) *From 'Passivity to Empowerment'*. RADAR, 25 Mortimer Street, London.

Forest, M. and Pearpoint, J. (1991) *Two Roads: Exclusion or Inclusion*. Toronto: Centre for Integrated Education and Democracy, McGill University.

Francis, D. (1987) *Unblocking Organizational Communication*. Aldershot: Gower.

Hall, J. (1993) 'The meaning of inclusion', *Learning Together Magazine* **6** (December), 19.

Halliday, P. (1989) *Special Needs in Ordinary Schools: Children with Physical Disabilities*. London: Cassell.

Harris, I. (1998) 'Missing the target', *Special Children* (September) 35.

Hirstle, E. (1995) 'A perfect baby and a much wanted son', in Cornwall, J. (ed.) (1995) *Choice, Opportunity and Learning: Educating Children and Young People Who Are Physically Disabled*. London: David Fulton Publishers.

Hornby, G. (1994) *Counselling in Child Disability: Skills for Working with Parents*. London: Paul Chapman.

Humphreys, K. (1992) *Unlocking the Evidence: Teacher Assessment*. Newcastle upon Tyne: University of Northumbria.

Jones, P. (1992) 'Psychology for disabled people', *Educational and Child Psychology* **9**(1).

Mason, M. and Rieser, R. (1994) *Altogether Better (From Special Needs to Equality in Education)*. Book and video produced by Disability Equality in Education and Charity Projects. London: Baring Foundation and Hobson's Publishers.

McGuinness, J. (1994) *Teachers, Pupils and Behaviour: A Managerial Approach*. London: Cassell.

Moses, Hegarty and Jowett (1988) *Supporting Ordinary Schools: LEA Initiatives.* Windsor: NFER-Nelson.

OFSTED (1996) *The Implementation of the Code of Practice for Pupils with Special Educational Needs.* London: HMSO.

OPCS (1989) *Surveys of Disabilities in Great Britian.* Social Surveys Division.

Prosser, G. (1992) 'Psychological issues related to having others mediate in your life', *Educational and Child Psychology* **9**(1).

Reindal, S. M. (1995) 'Discussing disability – an investigation into theories of disability', *European Journal of Special Needs Education* **10**(1), 58–69.

Rieser, R. (1994) 'An opportunity not to be missed: 1994 inclusive school policies', *New Learning Together Magazine* **1** (April).

Rieser, R. and Mason, M. (1992) *Disability Equality in the Classroom: A Human Rights Issue* (republished version). Disability Equality in Education, 78 Mildmay Grove, London N1 4PJ.

SCAA (School's Curriculum and Assessment Authority) (1996) Supporting Pupils with Special Educational Needs (Key Stage 3). SCAA Publications, PO Box 2235, Hayes, Middlesex UB3 1HF.

Schmuck, R. A. and Miles, M. (1971) *Organisation Development in Schools.* Palo Alto, CA: Mayfield.

SENJIT (Institute of Education) (1995) *Schools Policy Pack.* London: National Children's Bureau.

Stone, D. (1985) *The Disabled State.* London: Macmillan.

Thomas, G. (1997) 'Inclusive schools for an inclusive society', *British Journal of Special Education* **24**(3), 106.

Thomas, P. (1995) 'Curricular inclusion for assisted communicators'. Valence School, Westerham and Postgraduate Diploma (Physical Disabilities) Seminar. Christ Church College, Canterbury.

Tod, J., Blamires, M. and Castle, F. (1998) *Implementing Effective Practice.* London: David Fulton Publishers.

UNESCO *The Salamanca Statement for Action on Special Needs Education*, (obtained from UNESCO, Special Educational Programme, 7 Place de Fontenoy 7535, Paris 07-SP).

Warnock Report (1978) *Report of the Committee of Enquiry into the Education of Handicapped Children and Young People.* London: HMSO.

Webber, A. (1991) *Independence and Integration Series* (4 books of photo-copiable resource materials). Obtainable from the author via John Cornwall at Christ Church University College, Canterbury.

Further contact

John Cornwall (Senior Associate Lecturer and Research Psychologist),
Christ Church University College, Centre for Research in Education,
Canterbury, Kent CT1 1QU, UK.

John Cornwall (Director), ScopE (Education and Training), 20 The Ness, Canterbury, Kent CT1 3NL, UK. Phone: (0374) 275135. Fax/voicemail: 01227 470311.